Investing in Revolutions

Creating Wealth from Transformational Technology Waves

Tal Elyashiv

Investing in Revolutions: Creating Wealth from Transformational Technology Waves

Tal Elyashiv
Ramat Hasharon, Israel

ISBN-13 (pbk): 979-8-8688-1176-0 ISBN-13 (electronic): 979-8-8688-1177-7
https://doi.org/10.1007/979-8-8688-1177-7

Copyright © 2025 by Tal Elyashiv

Managing Director, Apress Media LLC: Welmoed Spahr
Acquisitions Editor: Shivangi Ramachandran
Development Editor: James Markham
Editorial Assistant: Gryffin Winkler

Cover designed by eStudioCalamar

Distributed to the book trade worldwide by Springer Science+Business Media New York, 1 New York Plaza, Suite 4600, New York, NY 10004-1562, USA. Phone 1-800-SPRINGER, fax (201) 348-4505, e-mail orders-ny@springer-sbm.com, or visit www.springeronline.com. Apress Media, LLC is a California LLC and the sole member (owner) is Springer Science + Business Media Finance Inc (SSBM Finance Inc). SSBM Finance Inc is a **Delaware** corporation.

For information on translations, please e-mail booktranslations@springernature.com; for reprint, paperback, or audio rights, please e-mail bookpermissions@springernature.com.

Apress titles may be purchased in bulk for academic, corporate, or promotional use. eBook versions and licenses are also available for most titles. For more information, reference our Print and eBook Bulk Sales web page at http://www.apress.com/bulk-sales.

Any source code or other supplementary material referenced by the author in this book is available to readers on GitHub. For more detailed information, please visit https://www.apress.com/gp/services/source-code.

If disposing of this product, please recycle the paper

Table of Contents

About the Author

Tal Elyashiv is an entrepreneur, venture capitalist, serial investor, author of the bestseller *Blockchain Prophecies*, and the founder and managing partner of SPiCE VC, the best performing blockchain venture capital fund. With a background as a senior executive and changemaker at both Bank of America and Capital One while also cofounding Securitize, the leading platform for tokenizing real-world assets globally, Elyashiv seamlessly combines traditional finance experience with his visionary leadership in deep tech. This unique expertise makes him one of today's preeminent voices and blue-flame thinkers on how to foresee, understand, and capitalize on the emergence and convergence of revolutionary technologies.

About the Reviewer

Liz Whelan has spent over two decades shaping narratives at the cutting edge of technology. From her early work as spokesperson for the world's largest wireless provider to guiding today's pioneering AI companies, she has consistently helped innovative firms translate complex technologies for mainstream audiences. Through LWPR Consulting, which she founded in 2008, she provides strategic communications counsel to companies driving transformation with today's most consequential technologies. Based in Chicago, Liz partners with leading organizations around the globe, helping them break through the noise and establish thought leadership in their respective markets.

Introduction

We stand at the threshold of what may be humanity's most transformative technological revolution. While the Mechanical Age gave us engines and machines, the Electrical Age powered our world, and the Digital Age connected us globally, the emerging Quantum Revolution promises something far more profound: the convergence of transformational technologies that will fundamentally reshape how we live, work, and interact with the world around us.

This isn't hyperbole. The integration of artificial intelligence, blockchain technology, and quantum computing—along with other breakthrough innovations—is already beginning to alter everything from how we diagnose diseases and wage wars to how we manufacture goods and manage global supply chains. The pace of change is unprecedented, with technologies reaching mass adoption in months rather than decades. Just consider that it took electricity 46 years to reach 50 million users, while ChatGPT achieved the same milestone in just two months.

Yet, this acceleration creates both opportunity and challenge. For investors, business leaders, and innovators, the Quantum Revolution represents perhaps the greatest wealth creation opportunity since the dawn of the Industrial Revolution. But navigating this landscape requires more than just understanding individual technologies—it demands insight into how these innovations converge and transform industries. Think of it as technological alchemy, where the combination of elements creates something far more valuable than the sum of its parts.

I've spent years in the trenches of technological innovation, watching promising technologies soar and watching others fade into obscurity. What I've learned is that success in this space isn't just about picking winners—it's about understanding the entire ecosystem of change. It's about recognizing patterns, identifying genuine inflection points, and most importantly, understanding the "force field factors" that determine whether a technology will flourish or falter.

This book provides a framework for understanding and capitalizing on this technological revolution. Drawing from historical patterns of previous technological revolutions while acknowledging the unique characteristics of our current moment, we'll explore how technologies mature, converge, and eventually reshape entire industries. We'll examine the roles different types of companies play in this evolution—from Originators who pioneer breakthrough innovations to Creative Destructors who reshape markets, and from Disruptive Innovators who reimagine possibilities to the Beneficiaries who scale these technologies to maturity.

Through detailed analysis of three critical sectors—healthcare, defense, and manufacturing—we'll see how these revolutionary technologies are already transforming major industries. These case studies offer practical insights into how investors can identify opportunities, time their investments, and build strategies that align with the trajectory of technological change.

But perhaps most importantly, this book emphasizes that successfully investing in revolutionary technologies requires more than just technical knowledge or market timing. It demands an understanding of the broader "force field factors"—the social, economic, regulatory, and infrastructural conditions that determine whether a technology will flourish or falter. Just as electricity required a complex ecosystem of power plants, transmission lines, and electrical devices to realize its revolutionary potential, today's transformational technologies require the right confluence of factors to achieve their world-changing potential.

Be warned, however. This isn't your typical investment book filled with hot stock tips or get-rich-quick schemes. Instead, it's a framework for understanding our new landscape of change and how to effectively capitalize on perhaps the most significant technological transformation in human history. It will also help you answer the most pressing questions as the Quantum Revolution continues to take shape: Will you be prepared to capitalize on this historic moment of transformation? Will you recognize the opportunities that others miss? Will you understand not just where technology is heading but how to position yourself ahead of the curve?

The revolution is already underway. The future belongs to those who can recognize the patterns of change and position themselves accordingly to capitalize on this historic moment of transformation. Let's begin.

CHAPTER 1

Understanding the Technology Evolution Cycle Through History

At the heart of every technological revolution lies a breakthrough that dramatically alters the human condition. Whether it's the fire that illuminated the path of early humans or the Internet that connected the globe in a web of information, revolutionary technologies share a common trait: they trigger a cascade of further innovations, transforming our lives, industries, and societal structures in profound ways.

These revolutions are not confined to mere technological advancements; they extend to material and ideological realms, impacting business management, education, social interactions, and finance. The productivity and efficiency gains they foster often lead to significant changes in human existence and culture.

Yet, while these phenomena create a cascade of innovations that follow them, these types of life-will-never-be-the-same technologies don't occur in a vacuum. Each leap forward is predicated on a foundation of existing systems and infrastructure, as well as a confluence of conducive factors that collectively determine the trajectory of a technology's adoption.

© Tal Elyashiv 2025
T. Elyashiv, *Investing in Revolutions*, https://doi.org/10.1007/979-8-8688-1177-7_1

For these technologies to transform the world, a complex interplay of macrofactors, which include social acceptance, geopolitical stability, economic viability, and societal readiness, is required. This force field creates an environment that will either elevate an innovation or have a hand in its demise. The macrofactors must be in place for success.

Albert Einstein once said, "Imagination is more important than knowledge. For knowledge is limited, whereas imagination embraces the entire world, stimulating progress, giving birth to evolution." (Calkin and Karlsen, 2014). Einstein's words highlight the value of imagination over knowledge by suggesting that while knowledge has its limits, imagination can explore boundless possibilities, fueling progress and leading to new developments. This principle underlines the importance of innovation and its capacity to alter the world. Yet, the transformation of innovative ideas into practical realities that significantly change our daily lives depends on collective effort, societal support, and favorable conditions. In the journey through transformative technologies, it's important to recognize that innovation's potential to achieve widespread influence is the result of collaboration and the merging of diverse contributions.

Equally as influential as the macrofactors in determining the "why" or "how" an innovation transforms into a revolution is understanding the adoption cycles that propel those technologies into the history books and our everyday lives forever. As with many emerging technologies, the journey from idea to invention, to widespread application is not linear. And in today's world, which is teeming with buzzwords and breakthroughs, understanding the essence of transformative technologies requires more than just surface-level enthusiasm. It demands a deep dive into the cycles of adoption that have historically reshaped society.

For the investor community, being able to identify the confluence of an innovation with its macrofactors and then knowing where it sits on its adoption cycle journey can provide a financial crystal ball ahead of a boom or a bust.

Technology Adoption Cycle

The journey of a technology from inception to ubiquity can be mapped through a series of stages, each marked by its own challenges and opportunities. This cycle, from innovators and early adopters to the early majority and laggards, is a dance of feasibility, utility, and perception. Yet, as we move through eras of technology revolutions, this cycle has gradually accelerated, influenced by globalization, digital connectivity, and a societal shift toward rapid gratification.

To fully leverage the potential of technology waves for wealth creation, one must grasp the dynamics of technology adoption. The cycle, often a tumultuous journey with its share of failures and successes, is crucial for assessing risk, potential growth, and timing for investment. At its core, this cycle is about understanding how innovations transition from niche ideas to widespread acceptance.

The Innovation–Adoption Curve is a graphical depiction of Diffusion of Innovations (Rogers, 1962), a model created by Ohio State professor Everett Rogers as a method of explaining how, why, and the rate at which an innovation spreads through a population or social system (Figure 1-1).

Rogers' Innovation–Adoption Curve or "Cycle" provides a framework for this understanding, categorizing adopters from innovators to laggards. Each group plays a distinct role in the diffusion of new technologies, influencing the speed and extent of their adoption. However, not all innovations smoothly sail through these stages; some encounter a chasm that can stall or even halt their journey to mainstream acceptance.

To understand how innovations transform from niche discoveries to revolutionary forces, we must first examine the pattern of adoption that characterizes successful technological transitions. The Innovation–Adoption Curve, developed by Rogers, provides a framework that has proven remarkably consistent across different technologies and eras.

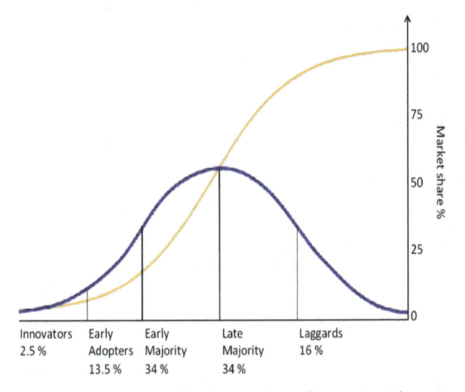

Figure 1-1. *The Innovation–Adoption Curve (Rogers Curve) Introduction: The Innovation–Adoption Curve, developed by Everett Rogers in 1962, illustrates the distribution of adopters for new technologies over time. The curve shows five adopter categories: innovators (2.5%), early adopters (13.5%), early majority (34%), late majority (34%), and laggards (16%). (Rogers, E. M., 1962)*

For example, the greatest modern example of a technology successfully "sailing" through Rogers' Adoption Curve is Apple's iPhone.

- *Innovators:* Tech enthusiasts who were quick to adopt smartphones when they were first introduced, despite high costs and limited applications.

- *Early Adopters:* Professionals and tech-savvy individuals who recognized the potential of having a computer in their pocket for both work and personal use.

- *Early Majority and Late Majority:* The general population adopted smartphones as they became more affordable and user-friendly, with an expansive app ecosystem.

- *Laggards:* Those last to adopt smartphones, often due to reluctance to change or lack of perceived need, until it became almost indispensable for modern communication.

But for every iPhone, there's a Google Glass.
Google Glass:

- *Innovators:* Technophiles who were excited about the prospect of wearable technology and augmented reality.

- *Early Adopters:* A small group that experimented with Google Glass for specific professional applications, such as medicine or manufacturing.

- *Failure Point:* The product never crossed the chasm to the early majority. High costs, privacy concerns, and lack of practical applications limited its appeal, leading to its discontinuation for general consumers.

Crossing the Chasm and Beyond

In *Crossing the Chasm*, Geoffrey Moore presents a nuanced adaptation of the traditional technology adoption life cycle, highlighting a critical gap that exists between early adopters and the broader market, often referred to as the "chasm." This concept elucidates why certain disruptive innovations fail to achieve widespread adoption, despite initial enthusiasm from innovators and early adopters.

However, Moore's analysis extends beyond the mere identification of the chasm. He argues that for revolutionary technologies to truly embed themselves in the fabric of society and maintain longevity, a comprehensive ecosystem encompassing applications, services, and ancillary technologies is essential. Furthermore, shifts in user behavior and consumption patterns are frequently necessary to facilitate this transition.

The adoption of innovations within industries and corporations underscores this complexity. Significant investments in research, the evolution of business processes, and adaptation to new business models are often prerequisites for the successful integration of new technologies.

Simply put, the wheel wouldn't have been the wheel without the concurrent development of the fixed axle to become truly transformative. In turn, the automobile would've never "taken off" without the invention of the internal combustion engine. These examples mirror the interconnected nature of technological advancement and adoption.

The Gartner Hype Cycle

The Gartner Hype Cycle represents a crucial analytical tool developed by Gartner, a leading research and advisory firm (Moore, 1991). It offers a graphical and conceptual overview of the life cycle of emerging technologies, charting their journey from introduction to mainstream adoption. This model is instrumental for businesses, investors, and technologists in understanding the development and maturation of new technologies, providing insights into their potential impact, adoption rates, and market viability. The cycle is divided into five distinct phases, each reflecting a different stage of a technology's acceptance and integration into society and markets:

1. *Technology Trigger:* The inception point of any new technology, characterized by initial buzz and interest. Innovations at this stage are often surrounded by significant media attention, speculative investment, and a focus on the technology's potential rather than its proven applications. It's a period of exploration, with startups and innovators racing to develop and deploy the first iterations of their products.

2. *Peak of Inflated Expectations:* At this juncture, success stories begin to emerge, alongside inevitable failures. The technology's potential applications and benefits are hyped to possibly unrealistic levels, attracting a flurry of interest from early adopters and speculative investors. However, the visibility often outpaces the technology's actual readiness or utility.

3. *Trough of Disillusionment:* Reality sets in as the technology fails to meet the high expectations set during the previous phase. Interest wanes as challenges in implementation, scalability, and performance become evident. Many initiatives falter or fail altogether, but those that persist start to find more practical and sustainable applications.

4. *Slope of Enlightenment:* As understanding of the technology's strengths and limitations grows, practical applications begin to emerge. The market starts to see the genuine value of the technology, leading to a more reasoned and realistic assessment of its potential. Businesses and early majority users start adopting the technology in useful and productive ways.

5. *Plateau of Productivity*: The technology achieves mainstream adoption, with clear use cases and value propositions. Its benefits are widely recognized, and it becomes a standard tool or practice within its target markets. At this stage, the technology's growth is typically incremental, focusing on improvements and expansion rather than radical innovation.

Understanding where a technology sits in its journey from inception to mainstream adoption is crucial for both innovators and investors. The Gartner Hype Cycle provides a valuable framework for mapping this progression, offering insights into the typical phases a technology traverses on its path to maturity.

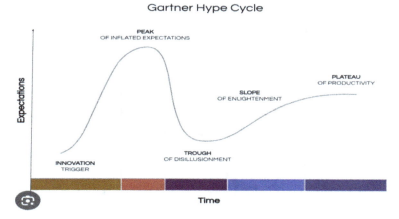

Figure 1-2. *The Gartner Hype Cycle represents the maturity, adoption, and social application of specific technologies through five phases. This visualization helps organizations understand technology's role in solving real business problems and exploiting new opportunities. (Gartner Research, 2023)*

Whether it's Rogers, Moore, or Gartner, these theories have much in common: tracing the journey of an idea from its genesis to widespread acceptance. They all reflect a dance between the tangible—such as the development of technologies—and the intangible, like the shifts in societal norms and expectations that drive and are driven by this progress.

The debate about whether these models (and which one) are valid is moot. None is "the gospel," and it is rare that an innovation tracks a model to the tee. Their contribution lies in providing us frameworks that help us ask questions and analyze an innovation against the ecosystem factors, along with a timeline, required for it to be adopted on a grand scale and thus revolutionary, and place it against a timeline.

The journey of an innovation is fraught with both triumphs and setbacks. As previously mentioned, for every iPhone, a marvel that seamlessly navigated through the stages of adoption, there's a Google Glass, a reminder of the challenges that lie in translating groundbreaking ideas into practical, widely accepted applications. For every VHS tape, there's the Beta.

These narratives underscore the critical importance of not just the technology itself but the ecosystem that supports it, including complementary innovations, services, and shifts in consumer behavior. The patterns of adoption are so much more than their graphical representations; they are reflections of our curiosity, drive to innovate, and resilience. They encapsulate the essence of progress—the tug-of-war between imagination and reality, vision and practicality.

When Mass Adoption Transforms into Revolution

As a technology reaches its zenith of mass adoption, it's poised to transform from a mere tool of convenience or efficiency into a cornerstone of societal transformation. This transition marks the evolution of a technology from widespread use to a revolutionary force, capable of reshaping the very fabric of how we live, work, and interact. It's at this juncture that innovations transcend their original applications, weaving themselves into the infrastructure of society and becoming so integral to our daily lives that their absence would be unimaginable. This metamorphosis signifies more than just the culmination of one cycle; it births a new era of sorts, where the technology in question catalyzes a fundamental shift in human capabilities, social structures, and economic paradigms.

In this moment of transition, we witness the adoption turn into revolution. It's a phase where the potential of technology to alter the status quo becomes palpable, promising not just incremental changes but a complete overhaul of existing systems. This transformative power redefines industries, revolutionizes communication, alters human behavior, and even reshapes social norms and values. Technologies that achieve this level of impact do not just serve as tools but become platforms for a myriad of innovations, fostering a cascade of advancements that extend far beyond their initial scope.

This pivotal phase is characterized by a synergy between technological maturity and societal acceptance, where the readiness of the technology meets the willingness of society to embrace change. It's a testament to the notion that true technological revolutions are not just about the technology itself but about how it is absorbed, integrated, and, ultimately, leveraged by society.

As we stand on the brink of such transformations, it becomes evident that these moments are not just endpoints but gateways to what's to come.

Eras of Revolution

To drive this point home more effectively, it's helpful to focus on three major technology revolutions and how they impacted the trajectory of modern history: the Mechanical, Electrical, and Digital Revolutions. While there are a variety of other examples that I'm sure historians, techno-anthropologists, and other experts could point to, each of these eras help us better understand their success and the force field of factors that made them so.

1. *The Mechanical Revolution*: Marking the onset of the Industrial Revolution in the late eighteenth and early nineteenth centuries, was characterized by the introduction of machinery to automate manual tasks, significantly enhancing productivity and changing the landscape of human labor.

2. *The Electrical Revolution*: Taking place in the late nineteenth and early twentieth centuries, was marked by the widespread adoption of electricity as a source of power, light, and communication, leading to significant advancements in technology and quality of life.

11

3. *The Digital Revolution*: Beginning in the late twentieth century and continuing into the twenty-first century, a shift from mechanical and analog electronic technology to digital electronics was made, leading to the creation and proliferation of digital computing and communication technologies.

The Mechanical or Industrial Revolution

The Mechanical Revolution, part of the broader Industrial Revolution, heralded a seismic shift in human productivity and the social fabric. This period was defined by the transition from manual labor to mechanized processes, underpinned by landmark inventions such as James Watt's steam engine, Eli Whitney's cotton gin, James Hargreaves' spinning jenny, and Henry Bessemer's "Bessemer Process." These innovations not only revolutionized their respective industries by drastically enhancing productivity but also set in motion a cascade of societal transformations that reshaped the landscape of labor, economy, and urban development.

This Mechanical Revolution was not an isolated wave of technological advancement but a critical component of the Industrial Revolution's complex landscape. At the heart of this revolution was a significant increase in population, driven by agricultural advancements that reduced mortality rates. This burgeoning population, migrating *en masse* to urban centers in search of employment, laid the groundwork for the industrial age, fostering a fertile environment for innovation and the exchange of ideas. The rise of a new middle class, wielding economic and political influence, further eroded traditional hierarchies, catalyzing changes in social structure that mirrored the seismic shifts in the economic landscape.

The Industrial Revolution was a complex story of how social, environmental, political, and economic forces converged in the eighteenth century to ignite an era of unparalleled growth and transformation. This unique amalgamation set the stage for the modern industrialized world.

While there were many breakthroughs during this period that can exemplify how a technology can alter the course of history if the force field of factors are firmly in place, Henry Bessemer's mid-nineteenth-century innovation is one of the more striking. Known as the "Bessemer Moment," Bessemer created a new process to make steel production more efficient, cost-effective, and scalable, facilitating the construction of railroads, modern infrastructure and catalyzing urbanization and the growth of new social classes.

Specifically, the Bessemer Process catalyzed a productivity surge by seven times, significantly reducing the cost of steel. However, it was in the United States where the process truly scaled up, driven by a surge in demand for steel following the Civil War, particularly for railroad construction. From 1864 to 1876, the United States saw the establishment of 13 factories employing the Bessemer Process, leading to an astonishing 87-fold increase in American steel production. As steel prices declined, its utilization expanded, making this invaluable material far more accessible.

Urbanization surged as steel became the skeleton of skyscrapers and the sinews of expansive bridges, fostering the growth of cities and the migration of populations to urban centers. According to data from the US Census Bureau (1975), New York City's population exploded from slightly over 500,000 people to 3.5 million individuals from 1850 up until 1900. Chicago grew from only 100,000 people to over 1.2 million during that same period.

This dramatic urban expansion is perhaps best illustrated by examining the population growth of America's largest cities during this period. The following data presents a striking picture of how the Industrial Revolution, enabled by innovations like the Bessemer Process, fundamentally reshaped urban landscapes.

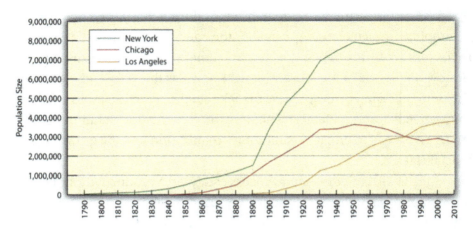

Figure 1-3. *Urban Population Growth in Major US Cities (1850-1900) Introduction: This visualization shows the dramatic population increase in major American cities, particularly New York and Chicago, during the latter half of the nineteenth century. (US Census Bureau, 1975)*

As workers flocked to these urban centers, steel underpinned the expansion of industrial capabilities and the creation of new industries, from automotive to construction, significantly contributing to GDP growth worldwide. Its versatility also permeated daily life, transforming transportation, housing, and consumer goods and setting the stage for the modern lifestyle.

As cities grew, so did their economies and the demand for energy. Urbanization led to a concentration of population and industries, creating massive demand for electrical power for lighting, manufacturing, and transportation. This demand spurred innovations in electrical generation and distribution, marking the end of the Mechanical Revolution and the onset of the Electrical Age.

The Electrical Revolution

The Electrical Revolution, as documented by Hughes (1983), fundamentally altered technology and improved quality of life across the globe. Edison's introduction of the light bulb in 1879 marked a crucial turning point (Israel, 1998), while Tesla and Westinghouse's development of the AC system revolutionized power distribution (Carlson, 2013), all of which set the stage for future innovations and societal transformations.

The telephone, invented by Alexander Graham Bell in 1876, revolutionized the way people communicated. For the first time, immediate and direct voice communication across long distances became possible, shrinking the perceived size of the world and facilitating faster decision-making in business and personal contexts.

The introduction of the light bulb by Thomas Edison in 1879 brought about a significant change in human activity, extending the day into the night and vastly improving safety and comfort in homes and workplaces. This invention was not just about displacing older light sources; it symbolized the potential of electric power to transform daily life, making activities independent of natural light cycles.

The widespread distribution of electrical power was made feasible through the alternating current (AC) system, developed by Nikola Tesla and George Westinghouse. This innovation solved the problem of transmitting electricity over long distances, making it practical and economical to electrify cities and industries far from power generation sites. The AC system was a cornerstone of the Electrical Revolution, enabling the creation of the modern power grid.

The backdrop for these technology's success was rooted in a mix of factors that, without them, may have led to a very different result. We assume that no matter what, the light bulb would've "crossed the chasm" at some point, but what made *this* moment possible?

Force Field of Factors Igniting an Electric World

In essence, the Electrical Revolution was the product of a moment in history where social desires, economic needs, geopolitical ambitions, and environmental considerations converged. The aftermath of the Industrial Revolution had ignited an insatiable appetite for further innovation. Society had tasted the fruits of technological advancement, leading to an increased demand for more efficient and effective solutions in both the workplace and daily life. This demand drove investments and interest in electrical technologies, seen as the next frontier for enhancing productivity and improving living standards. Plus, the burgeoning industrial landscape required more efficient energy sources to power machinery, factories, and transportation systems. Electricity offered a solution that was not only more efficient but also cleaner and more versatile than steam or coal power, enabling more refined and varied industrial processes.

However, even with forward-moving forces in play to propel the adoption of the light bulb (and electricity) forward, it faced similar challenges that many transformational technologies face—a lack of an infrastructure to support mass adoption. Thus, to reference the Gartner Hype Cycle, one could argue that the light bulb reached the "Slope of Enlightenment" and stalled there until the world around it could catch up. That's because creating a true transformation takes more than a single technology. For electricity, electrical grids to access homes and workplaces needed to exist, along with a host of other necessary "upgrades" to power a single lamp. Factories needed to be redesigned, and work itself had to be reimagined before electricity could begin to have a real economic impact.

The adoption of electricity followed a pattern that would become familiar in subsequent technological revolutions. The following graph illustrates how electrical infrastructure, despite initial hesitation, eventually achieved near-universal adoption in American households, setting the stage for countless innovations that would follow.

Electric power

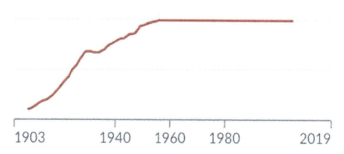

Figure 1-4. *Electricity Adoption Rates in US Households (1880–1940) Introduction: This graph illustrates the S-curve adoption pattern of electricity in American households, showing the initial slow uptake followed by rapid adoption in the early twentieth century. Source: US Department of Energy (2022)*

Once electricity reached "the Plateau of Productivity," it served as a catalyst for a host of technological innovations that transformed everyday life. While it's impossible to count the number of innovations born out of the Electrical Revolution, Thomas Edison's 2,332 patents can put its transformational power into perspective. The widespread adoption of electricity facilitated the creation of entirely new technologies that also achieved mass adoption within a generation or less, including the refrigerator, radio, washing machines, and the television (just to name a few).

It also brought about the computer—the technology that would usher in the next revolutionary era: the Digital Age.

The Digital Revolution

In the decades following the Electrical Revolution, the groundwork laid by these early electrical technologies facilitated the advent of computers and the Internet, kicking off the Digital Revolution—an era that saw the most rapid period of mass adoption of technology in our history.

According to data from the International Telecommunications Union (2023), computer adoption took less than two decades to reach 85% household saturation, while social media platforms achieved 80% saturation in less than a decade.

The acceleration of technology adoption rates represents one of the most striking features of the Digital Age. By comparing adoption timelines across different technologies, we can observe how the pace of technological integration has dramatically increased over time.

Figure 1-5. *Technology Adoption Rates Comparison Introduction: This comparative analysis shows the accelerating pace of technology adoption, contrasting the adoption speeds of various technologies from the telephone to social media. Source: Our World in Data (2023)*

The Digital Age, actuated by the PC, the Internet, mobile, and social media, echoed the transformative impact of the prior Revolutions but surpassed them in global reach and adoption speed.

Beginning In the late twentieth century, continuing to today, this era has fundamentally redefined societal communication, commerce, and community building. From the first email sent in 1971 to the global ubiquity of platforms like Facebook and YouTube, digital technologies have created a hyperconnected world, fundamentally altering how we interact, transact, and consume information.

The Digital Revolution can be distinguished by the transformative technologies at its core while also standing alone when it comes to the rapid pace at which these technologies have been adopted globally. This era has seen the barriers of distance and time collapse, enabling real-time communication and access to information on an unprecedented scale. Moreover, it has democratized content creation and dissemination, allowing voices from across the social spectrum to be heard.

The Five Pillars of the Digital Revolution

Characterized by rapid technological advancements and a shift toward an information-centric society, the Digital Revolution has been profoundly shaped by five key technologies: personal computers (PCs), the Internet, mobile computing, cloud computing, and social media. In the simplest of terms, these innovations have redefined work, life, and play. Once cannot exist without the other, yet each played a unique role in transforming the human condition—providing access to information, goods, and to each other like never before in history.

Personal Computers

In the early stages, personal computers (PCs) were seen as tools for hobbyists and enthusiasts, not essential household or office equipment. The transition to mass adoption was fueled by the development of more user-friendly operating systems (like Microsoft Windows), the decrease in prices, and the rise of software applications that catered to both personal and professional needs. The introduction of the IBM PC in 1981 and then the Apple Macintosh in 1984 made the PC a staple in homes, schools, and offices, marking its successful crossing into the early majority phase of adoption.

The growth of personal computing represents a pivotal chapter in the Digital Revolution. Historical data and projections reveal the remarkable trajectory of PC adoption, highlighting both its past impact and future potential.

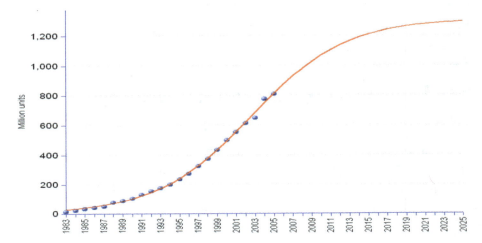

Figure 1-6. *Global PC Adoption (Historical and Forecast) Introduction: This chart presents both historical data and forecasted growth of personal computer adoption worldwide, showing the S-shaped adoption curve characteristic of transformative technologies. Source: International Telecommunications Union (ITU) (2023)*

The Internet

The Internet has been a truly transformative technology in every sense of the word, connecting billions of devices and individuals worldwide. It has dismantled geographic barriers, fostering global communication and collaboration.

Initially utilized by government and academic institutions for research and communication, the Internet crossed into mainstream use in the 1990s. The development of the World Wide Web by Tim Berners-Lee, the introduction of web browsers like Mosaic, and the establishment of an easy-to-navigate system of web addresses made the Internet accessible and useful to the general public. This, combined with the advent of affordable home computing, set the stage for the Internet's explosion into daily life, the enablement of new business models (e.g., e-commerce, gig economy), and the disruption of every traditional industry that existed.

The Internet's growth continues to reshape global connectivity at an unprecedented pace. Current projections suggest this expansion will continue well into the future, as illustrated by the following forecast of global Internet user growth.

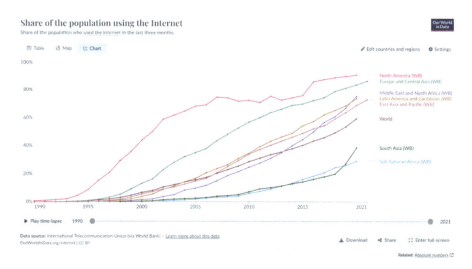

Figure 1-7. *Global Internet Users Growth (2024–2029 Forecast) Introduction: This projection shows the anticipated growth in global Internet users, forecasting an increase of 1.1 billion users between 2024 and 2029. Source: Statista Digital Market Outlook (2024)*

The global number of Internet users was forecast to continuously increase between 2024 and 2029 by 1.1 billion users (+16.92%). After the 15th consecutive increasing year, the number of users is estimated to reach 7.3 billion users and therefore a new peak in 2029.

Mobile Computing and Smartphones

Early mobile phones were primarily for voice communication, with some models offering basic texting capabilities. The launch of the iPhone in 2007 revolutionized the concept of the smartphone, offering a user-friendly interface, Internet connectivity, and a platform for mobile applications. The timing coincided with advancements in mobile Internet speeds (3G, followed by 4G) and a growing demand for mobile Internet access. These factors, alongside the development of the Android platform, propelled smartphones from a luxury item for early adopters to a ubiquitous part of modern life.

The smartphone revolution represents perhaps the most rapid technological adoption in human history. The following data illustrates how mobile computing has achieved near-ubiquitous status in a remarkably short timeframe.

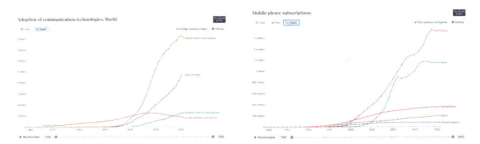

Figure 1-8. *Global Smartphone Adoption Rates Introduction: This visualization demonstrates the rapid adoption of smartphones globally, highlighting the unprecedented speed of mobile technology diffusion. Source: GSMA Intelligence (2023)*

Cloud Computing

Cloud computing has revolutionized how businesses operate by offering scalable, on-demand computing resources. Economically, it has lowered the barrier to entry for startups, democratized access to powerful computing resources, and spurred innovation in AI and big data analytics. Socially, cloud services have enabled a shift toward remote work, impacting urbanization patterns and work–life balance. Geopolitically, the centralization of data in cloud services raises questions about data sovereignty, privacy laws, and cross-border data flows, highlighting the need for international cooperation on cybersecurity standards.

The widespread embrace of cloud computing by organizations worldwide demonstrates how quickly digital infrastructure has become essential to modern business operations. The following statistics reveal the extent of this transformation.

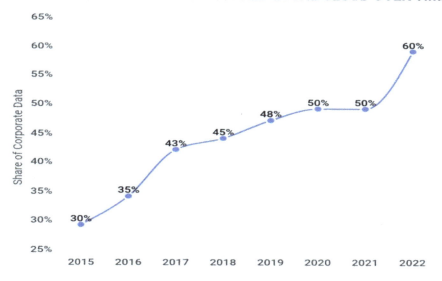

SHARE OF CORPORATE DATA STORED IN THE CLOUD OVER TIME

Figure 1-9. *Cloud Computing Adoption in Organizations Introduction: This figure illustrates the widespread adoption of cloud computing in organizations (O'Reilly, 2023) (Fortinet, 2021)*

Social Media

Social media platforms have redefined communication, enabling real-time, global interaction and content sharing—for good and bad. Platforms like Friendster and MySpace laid the groundwork for social networking, but it was Facebook's launch in 2004 that marked the true crossing of the chasm for social media. Facebook arrived at a time when Internet use was soaring, and there was a growing appetite for digital social connectivity. Its user-friendly interface, focus on real-life connections, and later, the introduction of mobile apps helped make social media an integral part of daily life for billions around the globe.

The explosive growth of social media platforms provides a compelling example of how digital technologies can achieve massive scale in remarkably short timeframes. The following visualization tracks this unprecedented expansion.

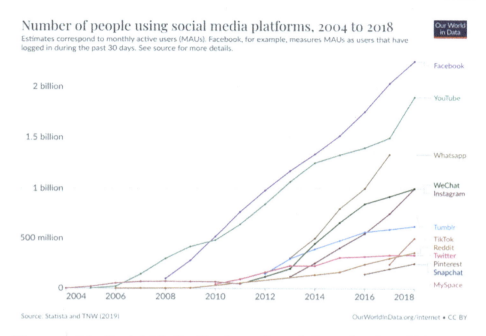

Figure 1-10. *Social Media Platform Growth Introduction: This chart tracks the growth trajectories of major social media platforms, demonstrating the rapid scaling of digital social networks. Source: DataReportal (2024)*

The Digital Revolution has not been without its challenges, igniting debates over privacy, data protection, and online freedom of speech. While international regulators and government officials continue to grapple with these complexities, the world (and technology) is looking ahead.

A Revolution in Transition or Twilight?

The Digital Revolution has been all about zeros and ones—binary code translating into everything from the ability to swipe right to the capacity to summon the entirety of human knowledge with a few taps on a screen. It has democratized information, upended industries, and even created new gods: the tech oligarchs. But as progress continues to march forward, the limitations of digital computing, bound by Moore's Law, have started to come into sharp relief.

Each technology revolution makes the next one possible. Hundreds of years ago, the invention of machines to automate laborious manual processes created the infrastructure to support the electricity that would power our world (and our devices) for over a century. Those devices and the vast innovations driving the Digital Revolution are the underpinning of the greatest shift in wealth, power, and knowledge the world has ever seen. But, as with all revolutions, it's not infinite.

We're standing on the precipice of our next transformational revolution—one that has been launched by the confluence of artificial intelligence (AI), decentralized ledger technology (DLT/blockchain), and quantum computing. Welcome to the Quantum Revolution.

The Rise and Fall of Technological Eras

The Digital Revolution is not twilighting because we've squeezed every last transistor onto a silicon wafer. Moore's Law, our technological North Star, is flickering out. Companies like Google and Microsoft are making their own chips because waiting around for the next big thing in silicon is a fool's errand. This isn't just evolution; it's a revolution in how we think about advancing technology.

This transition away from a one-size-fits-all tech approach marks a fundamental shift in how we interact with digital tools. The bar to entry for creating digital technology has plummeted, thanks to no-code platforms transforming coding from a wizard's craft to something more akin to a middle-skill job. And let's be honest, the latest smartphone isn't revolutionizing your life like the first one did. The frontier of innovation isn't in making a slightly better app—it's in leveraging digital prowess to crack codes in genomics, materials science, economics, and beyond.

It's about using bits to influence atoms. Take the Cancer Genome Atlas, for example. A project that began with the modest goal of sequencing tumor genomes now serves as a wellspring for breakthroughs in cancer treatment, demonstrating the power of digital technologies to drive forward the physical sciences.

The digital revolution, for all its disruptiveness, played a relatively minor role in the broader economy when compared to giants like manufacturing, healthcare, and energy. As we transition to this new era, the opportunity to impact every single sector, including manufacturing, healthcare, genomics, and energy, is monumental. Yet, capturing this potential demands not just technological innovation but a reimagining of what it means to innovate in the twenty-first century.

To use all the "tech cliches," there's a potential to "think differently" and move away from a world that celebrates "moving fast and breaking things" to one that recognizes the value of careful consideration and the pursuit of grand challenges.

The legacy of the Digital Revolution has provided the foundation for a new era of innovation in the Quantum Revolution.

It's All in the Name: Quantum Revolution

Why call our current technological revolution "The Quantum Revolution"? The answer lies in both historical context and the unprecedented fusion of transformative technologies we're witnessing today.

Historically, the term "Quantum Revolution" emerged in physics during the twentieth century, marking breakthrough discoveries in quantum mechanics that gave birth to transformative innovations like lasers, transistors, and semiconductors. The early twenty-first century saw discussions of a "Second Quantum Revolution," centered around emerging quantum computing and sensing technologies.

But today, we're experiencing something far more profound. The true Quantum Revolution transcends its physics origins, representing a fundamental shift in how technology shapes human existence. At its core is an unprecedented convergence: quantum computing fuses with artificial intelligence, blockchain, IoT, genomics, and autonomous robotics, creating a technological synergy greater than the sum of its parts.

This convergence isn't just about technological advancement—it's about exponential transformation. Just as quantum mechanics revealed that particles can exist in multiple states simultaneously, our current revolution enables multiple transformative technologies to interact and amplify each other's capabilities. AI enhances quantum computing, which in turn accelerates genomic research, while blockchain ensures security and trust, and IoT provides the nervous system for this new technological organism.

The result? A tsunami of innovation that fundamentally alters the human experience. This isn't merely another industrial revolution or digital transformation—it's a quantum leap in human capability and possibility. That's why "The Quantum Revolution" is more than just a nod to quantum physics—it's a recognition of the revolutionary, nonlinear, and transformative nature of our current technological era.

A Revolutionary Trio: AI, Blockchain, and Quantum Computing

These three revolutionary forces are set to join forces, promising to elevate each other's capabilities to unprecedented heights. These technologies, each formidable on its own, are poised to create a synergistic nexus that amplifies their collective potential, addressing the multifaceted challenges and opportunities of the digital revolution.

AI brings to the table its unparalleled ability to sift through vast data landscapes, identifying patterns and extracting actionable insights with efficiency and precision that mimic, and often surpass, human intelligence. Blockchain technology offers a robust framework for secure, decentralized transactions and the tokenization of assets, laying the groundwork for a new era of digital trust and data integrity. Together, they tackle critical digital era challenges, from ensuring data authenticity to managing the overwhelming torrents of data spawned by globally interconnected systems.

Enter quantum computing, the third pillar in this triad, with its transformative potential to process information at scales and speeds unfathomable to classical computers. Quantum computing introduces a new dimension of computational power, capable of solving complex problems in cryptography, optimization, and simulation far beyond the reach of current technologies.

The convergence of quantum computing with blockchain and AI heralds a synergistic amplification of their respective strengths:

The respective characteristics of each pillar of the Quantum Revolution address challenges caused by the digital revolution, which connected computer systems eventually created near-infinite amounts of data.

The intertwining of quantum computing with blockchain and artificial intelligence (AI) marks the dawn of a synergistic era, amplifying the unique strengths of each technology in a way that promises to redefine the landscape of digital innovation. The fusion of quantum algorithms with AI is set to dramatically accelerate machine learning processes, equipping AI with the capability to navigate more complex and nuanced problems. This combination is poised to usher in groundbreaking advancements in predictive modeling, natural language processing, and even artificial creativity, pushing AI's capabilities to new frontiers.

Simultaneously, quantum computing brings its transformative potential to the realm of blockchain, promising to fortify its security architecture against quantum threats and leverage quantum networks for unprecedentedly secure communications. This enhancement is not just about security; it's about efficiency too. Quantum computing stands to drastically improve the scalability and speed of blockchain operations, paving the way for a more agile and robust digital infrastructure.

Moreover, blockchain's role as a secure ledger for AI operations introduces a layer of trust and transparency previously unseen. By safeguarding the integrity and traceability of the data fueling AI systems, blockchain and AI together are laying the groundwork for decentralized AI applications. These applications promise not only enhanced trust in AI-driven processes but also the advent of transparent, tamper-proof decision-making frameworks.

When AI, blockchain, and quantum computing are woven together, they create a unified ecosystem characterized by secure, transparent data flows. This ecosystem is the bedrock upon which intelligent, ultraefficient applications and services can be built, potentially revolutionizing industries like finance, healthcare, and supply chain management. The promise of this ecosystem lies in its ability to deliver solutions that are not only secure and personalized but also deeply rooted in trust. Through the collective strength of these technologies, we stand on the brink of a new era of digital transformation, one that is as boundless in its innovation as it is grounded in security and intelligence.

But, like many groundbreaking technologies before them, blockchain, AI, and quantum computing are on a journey that requires navigating through a series of complex issues to fully realize their potential. Let's take a closer look at each one now.

AI: The First Pillar of the Quantum Revolution

Blockchain and AI stand on the shoulders of the Digital Revolution, leveraging the Internet, increasing computational power, and the proliferation of data as their pre-existing infrastructure. Blockchain's potential for secure, decentralized transactions promises to create new infrastructures for finance, governance, and identity, challenging existing power structures. AI, harnessing vast datasets and advanced algorithms, is creating infrastructures of automation and predictive analytics, transforming industries from healthcare to transportation.

Both of these technologies have been around for decades. In fact, after cracking the Enigma machine, which contributed to the defeat of Nazi Germany in WWII, mathematician Alan Turing (1912–1954) was fascinated about the possibility of creating a "learning machine" that could become artificially intelligent. In 1950, he famously published his "Turing Test"—a test of a machine's ability to exhibit intelligent behavior equivalent to, or indistinguishable from, that of a human. Some would argue that Turing's legacy to AI is equivalent to Benjamin Franklin's to electricity (Turing, 1950).

For years after Turing's breakthroughs, AI was only visible in universities and laboratories until the research of Prof. Geoffrey Hinton, a computer scientist and cognitive psychologist, and colleagues on multilayer neural networks in the 1980s created a clear model to use machine learning and deep learning (a subset of AI). I vividly remember my fascination and amazement at the AI wonders going through my first AI course as a Math and Computer Science undergraduate student in the mid-1980s. However, years passed until AI resurfaced.

So, why did AI essentially lay dormant for more than three decades? The technology was finally matched by data volumes and computational power. The conditions (or force field of factors) finally became ripe for AI's modern-era debut around 2013, when Prof. Hinton's neural networks startup, DNNresearch, was acquired by Google. But no one could have predicted (well, maybe some people) the explosion of AI onto the global lexicon than OpenAI's launch of ChatGPT. Only possible by using the treasure trove of data that exists online, ChatGPT changed the AI game forever.

Andrew Ng, chief scientist and leading deep learning researcher at Baidu Research, said in 2017, "AI is the new electricity. Just as 100 years ago electricity transformed industry after industry, AI will now do the same."

AI teases the boundaries of human cognition, promising breakthroughs in healthcare, education, and beyond. The possibilities of breakthroughs are, quite literally, endless. Yet, its path to mainstream adoption faces similar challenges to its technological predecessors—fraught with ethical dilemmas, concerns about job displacement, lack of societal and ecosystem readiness, and possibly the most profound question of what it means to be human in an age of intelligent machines. As Turing would surely advocate, the adoption of AI challenges us to balance innovation with humanity, progress with empathy.

Blockchain: The Second Pillar of the Quantum Revolution

In 2008, the world was grappling with the fallout of the largest financial meltdown since the Great Depression, trust in traditional banking systems was at an all-time low, and out of this chaos emerged an enigmatic figure—Satoshi Nakamoto. With a stroke of genius, Nakamoto introduced Bitcoin and its underlying technology, blockchain, to the world. It wasn't just a new form of digital currency being proposed but a revolutionary way to think about trust, transactions, and transparency in the Digital Age.

Blockchain is the embodiment of disruption. It's not merely technology; it's a challenge to the status quo, a rebuke to centralized authority, and a testament to the power of distributed consensus. Blockchain democratizes trust, taking it out of the hands of a few gatekeepers and distributing it across a network of nodes. This isn't just innovation; it's a radical reshaping of power dynamics, akin to the upheaval the Internet brought to information dissemination.

The story of blockchain, however, is a narrative rich with potential and fraught with complexities. It's about way more than just cryptocurrencies. Blockchain promises a new architecture for our digital infrastructure, from creating tamper-proof records of transactions to enabling smart contracts that execute automatically when conditions are met. This technology has the potential to redefine industries, from finance to supply chain management to healthcare, ensuring transparency, efficiency, and security.

Blockchain's power lies in its ability to decentralize and secure transactions, offering a new paradigm for trust and accountability. But with great power comes great responsibility—and in the case of blockchain, great risk. The decentralization that makes blockchain so appealing also presents challenges: scalability issues, environmental concerns due to the energy-intensive nature of mining, and the paradox of achieving widespread adoption without compromising its decentralized ethos.

The technology's capacity to empower individuals and communities by enabling decentralized applications and autonomous organizations is immense. Yet, this vision of a decentralized utopia is not a foregone conclusion. It requires thoughtful engagement with the technology, an understanding of its potential and pitfalls in a responsible way.

As we reflect on the history and trajectory of blockchain, it's clear that we're witnessing one of the most transformational technologies of our time. The true measure of its success will lie not in its technical achievements alone but in how it reshapes our societal structures, influences our economic systems, and, ultimately, reflects our values in the new Quantum Revolution.

Quantum Computing: The Third Pillar of the Quantum Revolution

In the early twentieth century, the foundational principles of quantum mechanics began to crystallize, thanks to the pioneering efforts of physicists like Niels Bohr, Werner Heisenberg, and Erwin Schrödinger. Their work unveiled a universe at the atomic and subatomic level that defied classical intuition, governed by probabilities and wave–particle duality. It was a paradigm shift, revealing a layer of reality where particles existed in multiple states simultaneously until observed. This was not merely academic; it was the unveiling of a deeper truth about the fabric of our universe.

Fast-forward to the latter half of the century, and we see these principles not just as abstract concepts but as the bedrock for a new computational paradigm. Theoretical proposals by Richard Feynman and David Deutsch suggested that a computer based on quantum mechanics could perform tasks no classical computer could feasibly achieve. They envisioned a machine that, by harnessing the principles of superposition and entanglement, could explore an exponentially greater number of possibilities at once.

The real turning point came in 1994, with Peter Shor's development of an algorithm that demonstrated a quantum computer's potential to factor large numbers exponentially faster than the best classical algorithms. This wasn't just a theoretical exercise; it had practical implications, particularly for cryptography, that underscored the power and potential of quantum computing.

Today, we find ourselves at a critical juncture in the evolution of quantum computing. Research and investment are burgeoning globally, as both nations and private entities recognize the strategic and economic implications of quantum supremacy—the point at which quantum computers perform tasks beyond the reach of the most powerful classical supercomputers.

Quantum computers harness the principles of quantum mechanics to process information in ways that classical computers cannot. This allows them to solve certain types of problems much more efficiently. Here are some examples that illustrate the potential power and applications of quantum computers:

- *Factorization and Cryptography*: Quantum computers can potentially break widely used encryption methods, such as RSA encryption, by efficiently factoring large numbers—a task that is prohibitively time-consuming for classical computers. Shor's algorithm, for instance, could enable a quantum computer to factor large numbers exponentially faster than the best-known algorithms running on classical computers.

- *Drug Discovery and Molecular Modeling*: Quantum computers could simulate molecular interactions at a level of detail far beyond what classical computers can achieve. This could revolutionize the field of drug discovery by making it possible to accurately model and understand complex chemical reactions, leading to the development of new medications and treatments with greater speed and lower costs.

- *Optimization Problems*: Many problems in logistics, finance, and materials science involve finding the optimal solution from among a vast number of possibilities. Quantum algorithms, such as the quantum approximate optimization algorithm (QAOA), are designed to tackle these optimization problems more efficiently than classical algorithms, potentially saving industries billions of dollars through improved logistics, portfolio management, and material design.

- *Climate Modeling*: The complexity of climate systems makes them difficult to model accurately with classical computers. Quantum computing could provide the ability to simulate the Earth's climate system with much higher precision, leading to better predictions of climate change impacts and more effective strategies for mitigation and adaptation.

The geographic distribution of quantum computing development reveals important insights about where this revolutionary technology is taking root. The following map illustrates the current landscape of quantum computing innovation.

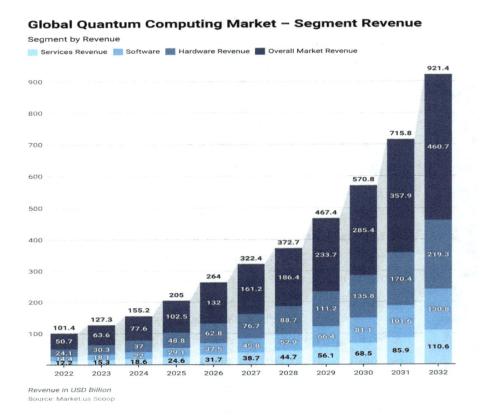

Global Quantum Computing Market – Segment Revenue

Segment by Revenue

Services Revenue   Software   Hardware Revenue   Overall Market Revenue

Revenue in USD Billion
Source: Market.us Scoop

Figure 1-11. *Global Distribution of Quantum Computing Companies Introduction: This visualization shows the geographic distribution of quantum computing development, highlighting North America's leadership in the field. Source: Boston Consulting Group (2023)*

North America is currently the epicenter of quantum computing, according to industry experts (Reuters, 2023). US companies building quantum processors include IBM, Amazon, Intel, Google, Quantinuum, IonQ, Microsoft, Quantum Computing Inc, and Rigetti Computing. In Canada, D-Wave Systems and Xanadu Quantum Technologies have been pioneers.

The Boston Consulting Group forecast reported that benefits of Quantum's data processing will begin to be realized as early as 2025 and have the potential to generate income of close to $1 trillion by 2035 (BCG, 2023).

The Accelerating Pace of Adoption Cycles in the Quantum Revolution

Marc Andreessen, the cofounder of Netscape and half of the famous venture capital firm Andreessen-Horowitz, said in 2003 "Any new technology tends to go through a 25-year adoption cycle" (Mecke, 2021).

While some would argue that we're still in the Digital Revolution, just the next phase of it, there is no argument whatsoever about the rapid pace at which new technologies are emerging and are achieving adoption.

There are many reasons for the accelerated timeline of turning concepts into reality. Geoffrey Moore recently attributed some of these shifts to the COVID pandemic. "The pandemic helped accelerate a global appreciation that digital innovation was no longer a luxury but a necessity. As such, companies could no longer wait around for new innovations to cross the chasm. Instead, everyone had to embrace change or be exposed to an existential competitive disadvantage" (TechCrunch, 2021).

Others believe that the consumerization of technology and its impact on the speed of diffusion, or complete disruption of adopter group roles (i.e., early adopters may now be middle school kids), may be what's at play. Or it's all of the above and more. Regardless, there is no doubt that the timescale of the technology adoption life cycle is shrinking.

The acceleration of technology adoption cycles represents a fundamental shift in how innovations spread through society. The following visualization captures this dramatic compression of adoption timelines across different technologies.

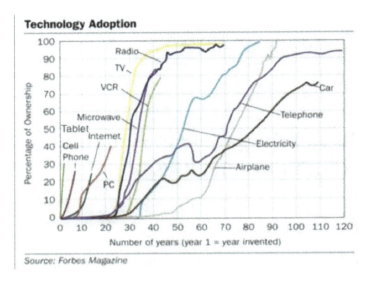

Figure 1-12. *Technology Adoption Timeline Compression Introduction: This figure illustrates how the time required for new technologies to achieve mass adoption has decreased dramatically over the past century. Source: World Economic Forum (2023)*

This accelerated timeline from idea to use case presents a landscape ripe with investment opportunities. Understanding the intricacies of the technology adoption cycle and the broader socio-economic impacts of technological revolutions is essential for investors looking to capitalize on these dynamics.

However, it's not just the speed of adoption that matters but the depth of integration into the societal fabric. The future is not just about technology; it's about the stories we tell, the values we uphold, and the world we aspire to create.

In an era where the cycle of technology adoption has been compressed to the blink of an eye, blockchain, AI and quantum computing stand as testaments to both the potential and peril of innovation. The journey of these technologies, from the fringes to the forefront, encapsulates the essence of our times—a period marked by rapid leaps of progress, yet shadowed by the complexities of ethical, social, and political implications.

The narrative of blockchain, with its roots in the desire for a decentralized ledger free from the constraints and vulnerabilities of traditional institutions, speaks to a deeper societal yearning for transparency, autonomy, and trust. Its potential to revolutionize industries, from finance to healthcare, is immense, yet its adoption is mired in a quagmire of scalability challenges, environmental concerns, and the inertia of established systems resistant to change.

AI, in contrast, offers a mirror to our own cognitive capacities, reflecting both our brilliance and our biases. Its adoption cycle is a dance with the very essence of human identity, challenging us to redefine the boundaries between the creator and the created. The promise of AI to augment human capabilities and address intractable problems is undeniable. Yet, its path is strewn with questions about privacy, ethical AI use, and the future of work in an automated world.

Incorporating quantum computing into this mix adds a new dimension—one of exponential power and speed. Quantum computing, with its roots in the principles of quantum mechanics, introduces an unparalleled computational power capable of addressing problems at grand scale. Its convergence with blockchain and AI could amplify their capabilities—enhancing blockchain's security and scalability and empowering AI with even more sophisticated analytical tools. Yet, the integration of quantum computing also brings its own set of ethical, security, and societal considerations, further complicating the narrative.

Navigating the ecosystem of blockchain, AI, and quantum computing adoption requires more than technological acumen; it demands a holistic understanding of the societal fabric into which these technologies are being woven. It calls for a narrative that resonates with the collective human experience, one that balances the excitement of innovation with a cautious appraisal of its impact.

The lessons of past revolutions loom large, reminding us that the true measure of innovation is not in the speed of its acceptance but in the depth of its integration into the human story.

Summary

It's crucial to recognize that the story being told isn't just about the acceleration of technology adoption; it's also about the remarkable pace at which new technologies are emerging. And it's not just about new devices. The innovations that have recently materialized are tremendously consequential and disruptive.

The profound implications of living in an era where the average person is exposed to orders of magnitude more technological advancements than someone half a century ago can be overwhelming, even for the most experienced technologist and investor. Consider the access to information, the analytical tools at our disposal, and the improved capacity to make informed investment decisions. We're not just passive observers of this technological tide; we're participants with the power to shape our futures.

Now, perhaps more than ever, there exists a tremendous value in cultivating the ability to discern true revolutions from mere noise. The converging dynamics that are enabling transformational technology waves are creating unprecedented opportunities for wealth generation, but the right skills and information to identify these transformative moments early and to make savvy investment decisions become indispensable. In an era defined by rapid technological progress and its societal implications, understanding the interplay between these forces is key to unlocking potential and forging a path to prosperity.

The sheer economic potential that lies in grasping the nuances of this new revolutionary age is truly remarkable. This isn't just evolution; it's a gold rush for those who know where to look.

CHAPTER 2

Identifying the Trends and Spotting the Next Big Wave

Well before a particular technology becomes mature enough to even begin its path toward adoption or "crossing the chasm," the force field of factors, along with the preceding developments that are essential for an innovation to take shape, comes into focus. The process in identifying the "what's next" and then analyzing whether or not the ecosystem surrounding that innovation is ripe for its successful proliferation is often referred to as technology foresight.

The significance of foresight cannot be overstated. As a fundamental element of success, foresight equips individuals and societies with the capacity to prepare for and navigate the future. The essence of foresight lies not merely in its ability to predict the future but in its power to enable proactive preparation and adaptation to forthcoming changes. In an era marked by unprecedented rates of change and shortened technology adoption cycles, technology foresight and the actions taken as a result of possessing it can reap tremendous rewards.

In human history, the ability to anticipate and prepare for future developments has always been a coveted skill. However, in today's world, characterized by rapid technological advancements, shifting job

© Tal Elyashiv 2025
T. Elyashiv, *Investing in Revolutions*, https://doi.org/10.1007/979-8-8688-1177-7_2

landscapes, evolving institutions, and changing values, foresight has become increasingly challenging to achieve. The pace of change is so swift that many feel disconnected from the future, unsure of what it holds and how to prepare for it. Contrary to this fatalistic viewpoint, foresight empowers individuals and organizations to shape their destinies actively. It involves thinking ahead, recognizing emerging trends and opportunities, and preparing to capitalize on them. Foresight is about seeing beyond the immediate, understanding the potential implications of today's actions on tomorrow's realities. It is this forward-looking perspective that enables people to navigate the turbulence of change and harness the opportunities it presents.

Foresight: A Skill for All or Superpower for a Few?

As the author, poet and journalist John Boyle O'Reilly once said, "Business, more than any other occupation, is a continual dealing with the future; it is a continual calculation, an instinctive exercise in foresight."

Great men and women with incredible technological foresight have dotted our historic landscape—garnering massive wealth and fame. One of the most celebrated figures in the world of technology and investment, whose foresight transformed not only his personal fortune but also the entire landscape of the Internet, is Jeff Bezos. In the mid-1990s, Bezos observed the rapid expansion of the Internet—an annual growth rate of 2,300% at the time—and envisioned a new way of commerce that leveraged this burgeoning platform. With a keen sense of where technology was headed, he founded Amazon.com in 1994, initially as an online bookstore.

Bezos's foresight didn't stop at simply selling books online; he saw Amazon as a starting point for what could become the "everything store," a concept far ahead of its time. He understood early on the potential of ecommerce before it became a staple of everyday life. This vision was grounded in the belief that the Internet would fundamentally change the way people shop, a belief that was, at the time, not widely shared.

Jeff Bezos's ability to anticipate and shape future technological trends didn't just make him one of the wealthiest individuals in the world; it also fundamentally altered consumer behavior, revolutionized retail, and established cloud computing as an essential part of the technological infrastructure of the modern world. But while Bezos's foresight was clearly remarkable, his grit, adaptability, and execution of strategy all played a critical role in his unprecedented success.

But you cannot talk about someone having remarkable foresight in recognizing the potential of an emerging technology without mentioning JP Morgan, who backed Thomas Edison's electric light venture. At the turn of the twentieth century, Morgan helped to establish General Electric, which became a dominant force in the electricity industry. In fact, Morgan had invested three hundred thousand dollars in the Edison Electric Light Company even before Edison had perfected his great invention (Gordon, 1989). That would be nearly $10 million in today's value. This move not only propelled Morgan to become a central figure in American capitalism but also significantly contributed to the electrification of America, thereby transforming the country's economic and social landscape.

While these individuals, who effectively leveraged foresight to create vast wealth, are excellent examples to showcase the most extreme cases of positive outcomes, foresight is not reserved for the oracles of the world. It's a universal power anyone can possess regardless of education, economic status, or experience. If a person has enough interest, is attuned to macro- and microforces around them, and has access to resources to enable greater understanding, effective foresight is well within their reach. And while it entails a bit of prophesying, foresight is a skill that is developed over time, becoming more and more precise and perceptive as its muscle is flexed.

Like mastering any skill, foresight requires practice, time, and sweat equity. The outcome doesn't have to mean the short-term accrual of billions of dollars but can offer the opportunity to better spot the right trends at the right moment to create wealth over the long run.

Foresight Is an Active, Not Passive, Pursuit

Cutting through the noise to uncover the harbingers of the next technological revolution is no small task, especially for those for whom this isn't their primary occupation. Yet, mastering the art of gathering and scrutinizing data is indispensable for those intent on pinpointing groundbreaking technologies worthy of investment. In a world where a deluge of new concepts, technologies, and startups emerges daily, possessing a robust understanding of the true potential of these ideas is paramount.

This book is not a "how-to" on investing in early-stage startups. Rather, it's meant to help investors of all types navigate the complexities of a new technological era that is rapidly progressing but is still young enough to offer immense opportunities for wealth creation. Your investment decisions will be informed by an array of publicly available information—information that has already been processed, vetted, and analyzed by a spectrum of industry experts, consultants, corporations, and analysts. While they lay the groundwork, the onus of filtering this data, evaluating varying perspectives, and employing critical thinking to arrive at astute investment choices falls on your shoulders.

Identifying opportunities to participate in this exciting revolutionary period is an active, not passive, pursuit. It demands an eagle eye for connecting disparate dots, an ability to read between the lines of prevailing narratives, and the vision to peer beyond the present buzz to gauge future implications. It's a journey that calls for perpetual curiosity and a willingness to immerse oneself in the deluge of innovation. In this race, the future doesn't wait; hence, neither can we.

Seven Ways to Hone Your Foresight

Now more than ever, in an age when new technology is being introduced more frequently and adoption cycles are condensed, those who can effectively leverage foresight to identify and invest in the next big technology breakthrough stand to gain a significant competitive advantage. The challenge, however, lies in distinguishing between fleeting trends and truly transformative technologies. The following sections examine the strategies investors can employ to harness foresight in spotting and capitalizing on emerging technological revolutions.

Continuous Learning and Curiosity

Curiosity may have killed the cat, but it is your friend when it comes to identifying technology trends.

The bedrock of elevating your foresight in technology and business lies in a commitment to continuous learning and an insatiable curiosity. This means actively seeking out the latest trends, breakthroughs, and developments that are shaping the fields of technology and business. However, true foresight also requires looking beyond the confines of one's immediate domain, exploring a wide array of disciplines to uncover how disparate trends might intersect and influence each other. Such a broad and deep approach to knowledge acquisition fuels the ability to anticipate future shifts and opportunities.

Consuming content from a diverse range of voices, from futurists dreaming up the next big thing to VCs betting big on startups, enriches your understanding. It's not just about what's new; it's about what's impactful, what challenges it poses, and how it's being adopted. Think beyond the obvious. Look for patterns, gaps, and opportunities that can inspire you to adopt or create new solutions.

Embracing curiosity means stepping out of your comfort zone, questioning established norms, actively seeking varied viewpoints, and being receptive to all kinds of feedback. Probe into the possible effects of a new technology—how it might alter business models, impact society, or redefine the human experience. Consider the risks, the costs, the intricacies of its integration. Look at who's leading the charge and who's on the sidelines. Determine where on the adoption curve a technology stands. Moreover, by observing the moves and strategies of key industry players, you can gather valuable lessons and anticipate future trajectories. Watching how these entities navigate technological advancements offers a lens through which to forecast and strategize your next steps.

Engage with the Innovation Ecosystem

Engaging with the innovation ecosystem is crucial for those looking to elevate their foresight in technology and business. This involves building robust relationships with thought leaders, innovators, and entrepreneurs who are at the forefront of their fields. By actively participating in tech conferences, webinars, and online communities relevant to your interests, you gain access to a wealth of early insights into emerging technologies and trends. Furthermore, collaboration plays a key role in deepening your understanding and exposure to new developments. Consider forging partnerships with startups, research institutions, or incubators. Such collaborations not only provide a front-row seat to cutting-edge research and development but also open up opportunities for hands-on involvement in pioneering projects. Together, these strategies of networking and collaboration within the innovation ecosystem serve as vital components in enhancing your ability to foresee and navigate future technological landscapes.

Building and nurturing connections with individuals who are at the forefront of innovation is crucial. Engaging with thought leaders, entrepreneurs, and forward-thinkers provides unique insights into the trajectory of technology and business. Furthermore, participating in communities—whether through forums, conferences, or discussions—where future trends are debated enriches one's perspective and sharpens foresight. These networks serve as invaluable resources for staying ahead of the curve.

Analytical Thinking

Enhancing your foresight involves sharpening your ability to sift through information critically, distinguishing between genuinely significant developments and those that are merely passing fancies. Scenario planning stands out as a vital instrument, allowing for the visualization of various potential outcomes that draw from existing trends. This process is not just about identifying what might happen but also entails a deep dive into the ramifications of these possibilities and formulating strategies to adeptly navigate the unfolding landscape.

For instance, consider the blockchain industry's evolution from a cryptocurrency-centric technology to a foundation for developing secure, decentralized applications across various sectors. Observing investments by major firms like BlackRock, Fidelity, JP Morgan, and others, along with the proliferation of startups in the blockchain space, can reveal the technology's maturing landscape.

In fact, Larry Fink, CEO of BlackRock, was vocal early on about the potential of blockchain and tokenization, stating that the tokenization of real-world assets (like digital securities, digital bonds, and tokenized stocks) "could revolutionize, again, finance."

Similarly, the rapid growth and investment in AI across industries—from healthcare, where AI is used for diagnostic purposes, to customer service, with chatbots providing 24/7 assistance—underscore AI's transformative potential. Monitoring patent filings in AI, significant funding rounds for AI startups, and endorsements by leading tech figures can guide your assessment of AI's trajectory.

Exploring the rise of EVs provides another example. The shift in investment patterns toward EV and battery technology companies, government policies supporting EV adoption, and automotive giants announcing transitions to electric fleets signal a significant industry transformation. Analyzing these movements, along with market projections by entities like Bloomberg New Energy Finance, can inform a strategic foresight approach.

If you're equipped with the resources and expertise to directly analyze a technology, you're at an advantage. However, for many, adopting the role of an investigator becomes essential. This means delving into the market or industry's response to a technology, listening to what experts are articulating, and critically observing their actions—for actions often convey more than words. It's crucial to identify who is investing in the technology, which startups are receiving funding and from whom, and who is dedicating efforts toward research and patenting activities around the technology. Assess whether the touted use cases represent groundbreaking innovations or merely incremental improvements. Seek insights from authoritative sources like Gartner or Forrester to gauge the technology's potential. Understanding the current market size, adoption rates, and future growth projections, including the compound annual growth rate (CAGR) over the next five to ten years, can provide a solid foundation for your foresight.

Through this meticulous process of investigation and analysis, you gain not just a predictive outlook but a comprehensive understanding of how a technology might reshape the industry, influence market dynamics, and offer real value beyond the hype.

Leverage Tools and Resources

When you're researching cutting-edge technology, cutting-edge resources and tools to complete the task are crucial. Data analytics, AI, and various technological instruments are key in unearthing emerging patterns and seizing nascent opportunities. Moreover, grounding your analysis in information from reputable sources and industry reports ensures that your foresight is both accurate and comprehensive, thereby facilitating more targeted and strategic decision-making processes.

To navigate this data-rich environment effectively, several tools stand out for their capacity to signal early trends:

- *Google Trends:* A go-to for many, Google Trends offers insights into the popularity of search queries over time. By inputting any topic of interest, users can gauge its historical search volume and even compare it against other trends, making it a valuable tool for validating the relevance and trajectory of specific subjects.

- *Exploding Topics:* This tool specializes in uncovering trends that are quietly gaining momentum, potentially indicating areas of long-term growth. Exploding Topics goes beyond merely highlighting what's currently in vogue by providing an analytical lens through which to view emerging phenomena.

- *Trends.co:* Specifically tailored for business professionals conducting market research, Trends.co serves as a comprehensive trend discovery platform. Its "Signals" feature categorizes trends and offers detailed reports, making it particularly useful for entrepreneurs looking to capitalize on business trends poised for substantial growth.

- *Podcast Notes:* Given the vast array of podcasts available, keeping up with them can be daunting. Podcast Notes offers a solution by allowing users to efficiently scan through thousands of podcast episodes for trend-related content. While it requires users to actively search for topics, it's an excellent resource for diving deeper into areas of interest that might not be as readily apparent in other media.

Additional tools and resources worth exploring include the following:

- *Crunchbase:* Ideal for tracking startups, funding rounds, and industry news, Crunchbase is invaluable for anyone looking to understand the investment landscape and identify companies at the forefront of innovation.

- *CB Insights:* For those seeking a data-driven approach to identifying trends, CB Insights offers market intelligence on emerging technologies and industries. Its reports and newsletters provide deep dives into sectors experiencing significant transformation.

- *Social Media Listening Tools:* Platforms like Brandwatch and Talkwalker allow users to monitor social media conversations around specific keywords, enabling the identification of trends as they emerge in real-time conversations.

Leveraging these tools equips you with a multifaceted approach to trend identification, combining quantitative data analysis with qualitative insights. By embracing a diverse toolkit, you enhance your capacity to foresee industry shifts, adapt strategies accordingly, and position yourself advantageously in an ever-evolving market landscape.

Embrace Experimentation

Embracing experimentation is a critical aspect of cultivating foresight, particularly in the context of technology and business. It's about much more than merely observing trends from a distance; it's about "diving in" and immersing oneself in the innovations that spark interest. This proactive approach allows for a deeper understanding of emerging technologies and business models, providing insights into how they operate, their potential impact on the world, and the new markets they could create.

To truly grasp what new innovations are and how they might reshape industries or society, engaging directly with these technologies is essential. This means moving beyond theoretical knowledge to hands-on exploration and application. By experimenting with new technologies, you gain a firsthand understanding of their capabilities, limitations, and possible applications in real-world scenarios:

- *Start Small and Play Around:* Regardless of how complex a technology appears to be out in the wild, you can begin experimenting with new technology in small and simple ways. For example, exploring AI and blockchain technologies can be a hands-on experience for everyday people, moving beyond theoretical understanding to practical application.

  For AI, you can start by engaging with AI tools that are becoming increasingly integrated into our daily lives. For example, using voice-activated assistants like Alexa or Google Home for tasks can familiarize one with AI's capabilities and limitations. Another practical approach is utilizing AI-based apps for personal finance management or health tracking, which can provide a deeper understanding of how AI processes data to make recommendations or predictions. Experimenting with AI-driven customer service, like chatbots on various websites, can also offer insights into how AI is revolutionizing interaction and problem-solving in the service sector. Even writing an email using ChatGPT can familiarize you with the practicalities of AI, which will only grow over time.

  When it comes to blockchain, the first step could be setting up a digital wallet and acquiring a small amount of cryptocurrency to understand the process of transactions on the blockchain. Participating in NFT (nonfungible token) marketplaces could provide a hands-on understanding of ownership and transfer of digital assets. Those interested can also explore blockchain's use in supply chain management by tracing products from origin to consumption, which some companies now offer as part of their consumer transparency initiatives.

- *Engage with Communities and Attend Relevant Events:* Engaging with communities is a fundamental part of familiarizing oneself with new technologies. It's through such engagements that individuals can gain firsthand experience, insight, and a shared understanding that can't be achieved in isolation. Community engagement in technological adoption involves connecting with groups and individuals who share your interest in a particular technology. This could mean joining online forums or local clubs where you can exchange ideas, experiences, and resources with like-minded people.

   Attending events like conferences, workshops, or meetups dedicated to specific technologies provides a platform to hear from experts, network with industry peers, and even discover opportunities for collaboration. It's also important to keep abreast of the latest developments through publications, whether these are scholarly articles from the *Harvard Business Review*, business-focused editorials from the likes of *Bloomberg* or the *Wall Street Journal*, or tech blogs like *CoinDesk* and *TechCrunch* that discuss the nuances and practical applications of the technology in question.

- *Skill Development*: Participate in workshops or online courses to learn about blockchain or AI. Platforms like Coursera or edX offer courses that can help you understand these technologies and their applications.

For an everyday person or a small retail investor, these activities are essential for demystifying complex technologies and enabling practical, hands-on learning. The collaborative nature of community engagement not only helps to break down barriers to understanding but also fosters an environment where new applications of technology can be imagined and realized.

Embrace a Growth Mindset

Elevating foresight requires a fundamental shift in mindset. This entails maintaining an openness to unconventional ideas and being prepared to challenge the status quo. Cultivating a clear vision of the future guides one's efforts in foresight, providing a direction toward which all insights and innovations are aimed. This visionary approach, combined with openness, is what ultimately enables individuals to not just anticipate the future but to actively shape it.

Cultivating a mindset that welcomes change and sees potential in uncertainty is crucial. Investors should view rapid technological and market changes as opportunities rather than threats. This perspective encourages adaptability, driving investors to continuously seek out and support innovations that could define the next wave of technology.

- *Embrace Failure As a Learning Opportunity:* When a new tech investment doesn't perform as expected, instead of seeing it as a loss, analyze what went wrong and what it teaches about market trends or technological viability.

53

- *Challenge Your Own Assumptions:* Actively seek out information that contradicts your current beliefs about certain technologies or investments to understand different perspectives and possibilities. Engage in discussions with individuals who have opposing views to expose yourself to new ideas and challenge your own status quo.

- *Adopt a Versatile Approach to Problem-Solving:* When faced with a challenge, whether it's a technological hurdle or an investment decision, brainstorm multiple solutions rather than sticking to conventional methods.

- *Set Stretch Goals:* Aim for objectives that push you out of your comfort zone, such as investing a small amount in an emerging technology you're learning about or developing a new skill relevant to future tech trends.

- *Reflect Regularly on Your Progress and Adapt:* Keep a journal or log of your learning and investment journeys, noting not just successes but also areas for improvement and adjustments in strategy. Use this reflection as a basis for setting new, more challenging goals that accommodate the rapidly changing tech landscape.

Learn from the Past

Learning from the past by conducting historical analyses of technology adoption and market evolution patterns is indispensable for shaping future investment strategies. This approach not only unveils patterns and triggers of technological success or failure but also provides a framework for understanding the dynamics of market disruptions. By dissecting the life cycle of past technologies—from inception through hype, adoption, maturity, and, in some cases, obsolescence—investors can gain insights into the factors that have historically influenced technological advancement and market acceptance.

Technological innovations do not exist in a vacuum; their success or failure is often tied to a complex mix of factors including timing, societal need, economic viability, and the existing technological ecosystem. For instance, the dot-com bubble of the late 1990s and early 2000s offers lessons on the importance of sound business models, even in the face of groundbreaking technology. Conversely, the eventual ubiquity of smartphones after earlier, less successful attempts at mobile Internet devices highlights the critical role of technological readiness and user experience in determining a technology's success.

Market disruptions often follow identifiable patterns, where emerging technologies displace established ones, creating new markets and value networks. The rise of digital photography and the subsequent decline of film-based photography is a classic example. This shift did not happen overnight but was the result of gradual improvements in digital technology, changes in consumer behavior, and the advent of new platforms for sharing photographs. Studying these patterns helps investors identify early signs of potential disruptions in current markets.

Let's illustrate these strategies with some examples:

- *Artificial Intelligence (AI)*: The rise of AI was predicted by industry experts in the early 2010s who noticed advances in machine learning and neural networks. A surge in VC investments in AI startups was another indicator of the impending AI wave.

- *Internet of Things (IoT)*: The IoT trend was identified at tech conferences and expos such as the Consumer Electronics Show (CES), where companies unveiled a range of smart, interconnected devices. By CES 2012, IoT had emerged as a central theme.

- *Blockchain Technology*: The advent of blockchain technology was signaled by the launch of Bitcoin, which officially took place on January 3, 2009, and the subsequent growth of startups and companies in the blockchain space.

- *Electric Vehicles (EVs)*: Initial Patent filings by companies like Tesla (2006), Nissan (1998), and GM (1996) hinted at a shift toward EVs. Simultaneously, governments in several countries announced initiatives to phase out internal combustion engine vehicles, bolstering the case for EVs.

Consciously Questioning "What's Next?"

The ability to anticipate and navigate the technological waves that shape our future is an indispensable skill in the arsenal of anyone looking to make informed, strategic investment decisions. As we stand at the crossroads of numerous emerging technologies, the question of "what's next?" is not merely speculative but a call to diligent exploration and action that's only possible through conscious, purposeful awareness about ourselves and the world around us.

For investors, the journey through technology foresight is a foundation upon which to build a robust strategy for identifying and capitalizing on the next big wave of innovation. It challenges us to look beyond the immediate horizon, to sift through the noise of the present, and to discern the signals that herald transformative change. This is not a passive endeavor but an active pursuit that requires a blend of curiosity, analytical rigor, and strategic thinking.

The narratives and strategies outlined serve as a primer, equipping you with the insights to not just follow trends but to lead in identifying and leveraging them.

Summary

In the race to capture tomorrow's opportunities, foresight is more than just a skill—it's an active pursuit that demands engagement, analysis, and the courage to act. While well-known business legends like Bezos and Morgan remind us of foresight's transformative power, their stories reveal a deeper truth: the future doesn't belong to prophets but to those who learn to read its signals.

The seven pathways presented here—from cultivating curiosity to embracing experimentation—aren't just strategies; they're the building blocks of technological prescience. They transform the overwhelming pace of innovation from a threat into an opportunity, converting information overload into actionable insight. Because in an age where technology evolves at breakneck speed, the ability to spot the next wave before it crests isn't just valuable—it's vital.

CHAPTER 3

Exponential Growth and the Laws That Drive Innovation

We are currently navigating an era of technological advancement so rapid and profound that it is without precedent in the history of mankind. Each day, we awake to a world slightly altered by new technologies that push the boundaries of what we thought possible. From the unfathomable depths of quantum computing, which promises to solve problems that today's best computers couldn't crack in a millennium, to the intricacies of artificial intelligence, soon to reach and exceed the complexities of true human intelligence, we are not just witnesses to but participants in a remarkable epoch. This period is extraordinary not merely for the speed of change but for the expanding breadth of possibilities these technologies can and will unleash.

It is estimated that humanity could advance more in just this century than over the past 20,000 years. Others compress that timing to just this decade. Regardless of predictions, this chapter examines how the technology that we're creating and enabling now is growing at an exponential rate.

© Tal Elyashiv 2025
T. Elyashiv, *Investing in Revolutions*, https://doi.org/10.1007/979-8-8688-1177-7_3

Defining Exponential

But what does "exponential" mean in terms of our lived experience and our ability to identify and capitalize on opportunities? As legendary futurist, author, inventor, and Google executive, Ray Kurzweil stated while describing his thesis of accelerated returns, "The reality of information technology is it progresses exponentially. 30 steps linearly gets you to 30. One, two, three, four, step 30 you're at 30. With exponential growth, it's one, two, four, eight. Step 30, you're at a billion."

To put this into clearer perspective, in 1909, Count Ferdinand von Zeppelin, the German general and inventor of the Zeppelin rigid airships, laid out a foundation for today's interconnected world by founding the very first airline. It took this innovation 64 years to reach 50 million users (Figure 3-1). It took about the same number of years for cars to reach the same milestone, more than 45 years for electricity, 14 years for computers, 7 years for the Internet, and about 4 years for Facebook. However, it only took two months for ChatGPT to reach 50 million users—shattering all previous records.

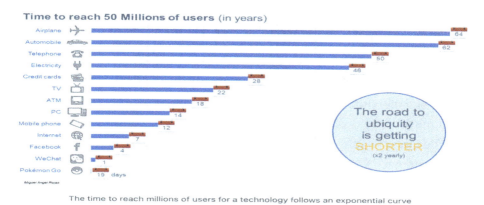

Time to reach 50 Millions of users (in years)

The time to reach millions of users for a technology follows an exponential curve

Figure 3-1. *Technology Adoption Rates (1900–2023): A comparative timeline showing the accelerating pace of technology adoption, tracking the time required to reach 50 million users across different innovations. The visualization spans from early transportation technologies requiring 64 years for adoption to modern platforms like ChatGPT reaching the same milestone in just 2 months. (Morgan Stanley Research, 2023)*

The interpretation of recent history can be misleading however. Technological progression often imitates an S-curve, marked by periods of slow growth, swift expansion, and ultimate stabilization. If we direct our attention merely toward the current phase, we might dismiss the impending exponential leaps. The epoch spanning from 1995 to 2007 observed the emergence of the Internet and tech giants like Microsoft, Google, and Facebook. This era also marked the introduction of cell phones and smartphones, signaling a phase of explosive growth. Yet, the span from 2008 to 2015 might seem less revolutionary. However, in truth, we may be standing on the threshold of a transformative phase never before experienced.

The Laws of Exponential Growth

The phenomenon of exponential growth in technology—the life cycle from innovation to ubiquity—has been compressed at a pace never before experienced in human history. But what does this acceleration mean for investors and society as a whole?

The laws of exponential growth capture how technology isn't just progressing; it's accelerating. Today, we see innovations rapidly build upon one another, creating a multiplier effect. What once took decades to move from invention to widespread use now happens in a few years—or even months.

This compression is due to technologies improving at an exponential rate, where each step forward is significantly larger than the last. Unlike the linear progression of the past, where each step was roughly the same size, today's growth is more like a steeply rising curve fueled by several factors:

- *Digital Technology:* Unlike physical products, digital technology can be easily and quickly scaled without the same manufacturing and distribution limitations.

- *Global Connectivity:* With the Internet, innovations can spread globally almost instantly.

- *Computing Power:* As computing power grows exponentially, it accelerates the rate at which new technologies can be developed and complex problems can be solved.

- *Data Availability:* The vast amounts of data we generate can train AI systems much faster and more comprehensively than ever before.

- *Interdisciplinary Innovation:* Technology no longer advances in isolation; breakthroughs often occur at the intersection of disciplines, amplifying growth.

It's not merely that innovation is happening faster; it's that each innovation catalyzes subsequent developments, shortening the path between idea and adoption even further. To understand how to harness the moment we're experiencing now, and the many micromoments of explosive innovation, it's worth taking a look at our three current "laws" of growth and how breaking them may be the key to true enlightenment.

Law #1: Metcalfe's Law and the Network Effect

The network effect, a principle where the value of a service increases with each additional user, profoundly impacts modern technology and society (Figure 3-2). We've seen this phenomenon play out with platforms like Facebook and LinkedIn, where every new user enhances the value of these networks exponentially, not just by adding themselves but by bringing their entire suite of connections. This interconnectedness accelerates the platforms' growth and their utility, making them more valuable and integral to users.

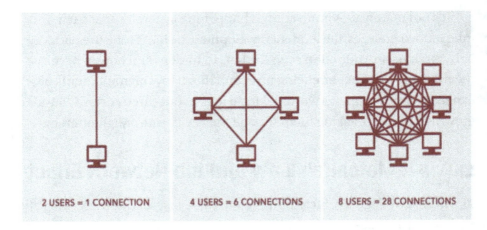

2 USERS = 1 CONNECTION   4 USERS = 6 CONNECTIONS   8 USERS = 28 CONNECTIONS

Figure 3-2. *Network Effect Value Multiplication: A visual representation of Metcalfe's Law demonstrating how network value grows exponentially as users are added to a system. The diagram maps the compounding effect of connections in digital networks, where value increases proportionally to the square of user numbers. (Metcalfe & Gilder, 2013)*

Today's social media platforms serve as vast ecosystems for the rapid spread of information and swift adoption of innovations. Each participant in these networks doesn't just contribute to but multiplies the reach and impact of every shared piece of information, leveraging their extensive connections. This dynamic is dramatically reshaping how quickly new technologies become known and are adopted across global populations.

Metcalfe's Law, named after Robert Metcalfe, the coinventor of Ethernet, quantifies this phenomenon (Metcalfe, 1995). It suggests that the value of a network is proportional to the square of the number of its users. Originally applied in telecommunications, this law is now a cornerstone in understanding the explosive growth of digital and decentralized networks, such as cryptocurrencies and blockchain technologies. In these systems, the network's utility and value escalate as more users join, enhancing the potential for transactions and interactions.

The Digital Age has turbocharged this network effect. The omnipresence of mobile technology, combined with an insatiable appetite for real-time information—be it through social media, live streaming, or instant messaging—ensures that once a new technology emerges, if it is perceived as valuable or innovative, it quickly captures the public's attention. The role of influencers in these networks can amplify this effect, turning new gadgets or ideas into predominant trends almost overnight.

Law #2: Moore's Law

Moore's Law, a principle articulated by Gordon Moore, cofounder of Fairchild Semiconductor and Intel, in 1965, observes that the number of transistors on a microchip doubles approximately every two years, while the cost of computers halves (Moore, 1965).

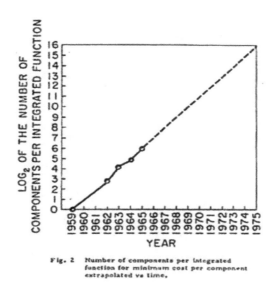

Fig. 2   Number of components per integrated function for minimum cost per component extrapolated vs time.

Figure 3-3. *Transistor Density Evolution (1971–2021): A logarithmic graph tracking Moore's Law through five decades, showing the exponential increase in transistor density on integrated circuits. The data validates Moore's prediction of transistor counts doubling approximately every two years. (Intel Corporation, 2022)*

This observation has not merely been a predictor of technological progression; it has served as a cornerstone for strategic planning within the semiconductor industry. Moore's insight has held true for decades, powering an era of unprecedented growth in computational technology, enhancing performance, and enabling the miniaturization of circuits.

The implications of this exponential increase in computational power extend far beyond the confines of technology itself. Consider the smartphone—a device that now outstrips the computing capabilities of the Apollo XI's onboard computers, instrumental in the 1969 moon landing. This example is a testament to the transformative impact of Moore's Law on everyday technology.

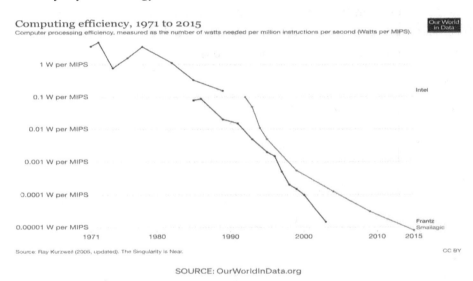

SOURCE: OurWorldInData.org

Figure 3-4. *Computing Power Comparison: Smartphone vs. Apollo Mission: A comparative analysis displaying the vast difference in computing power between a modern smartphone and the Apollo XI mission's guidance computer, highlighting the dramatic advancement in processing capabilities over five decades. (NASA Historical Archives & Apple Inc., 2023)*

Moreover, the digitization of information, which has become pervasive across all forms of media today, interacts synergistically with Moore's Law. Once information is digitized, it transcends physical constraints, becoming instantly accessible and shareable across the globe at breathtaking speeds. This transformation has turned digitized products and services into what we now recognize as exponential technologies, continually expanding in capabilities and potential applications at a rate once unimaginable.

Law #3: Kurzweil's Law of Accelerating Returns

The concept of exponential technology, as explored by visionaries like Ray Kurzweil, suggests that technological advancement doesn't just march forward; it leaps. According to Kurzweil, each generation of technology arrives faster than the previous, growing more powerful and simultaneously decreasing in cost.

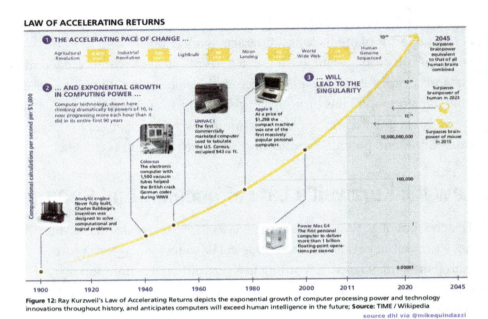

Figure 12: Ray Kurzweil's Law of Accelerating Returns depicts the exponential growth of computer processing power and technology innovations throughout history, and anticipates computers will exceed human intelligence in the future; **Source:** TIME / Wikipedia

source dhl via @mikequindazzi

Figure 3-5. *Kurzweil's Law of Accelerating Returns: An exponential curve depicting the accelerating rate of technological advancement as theorized by Ray Kurzweil, showing how each technological breakthrough enables faster subsequent innovations. (Kurzweil, 2005)*

One might wonder about the economics of such rapid advancement. Does doubling the performance of technology necessarily mean a proportional increase in cost? Surprisingly, no. Consider the evolution of mobile phones: over the past decade, while their prices have not quite doubled in the United States, their performance has skyrocketed.

Take 3D printing, for instance, where costs plummeted by 400 times in just 7 years. Solar technology followed a similar trajectory, with costs reducing by 200 times over 2 decades. Drones and genomic sequencing have also seen dramatic reductions in cost, with the price of sequencing a human genome dropping from $100 million to just over $1,000 in 16 years.

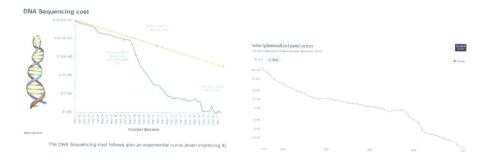

Figure 3-6. *Cost Reduction in Emerging Technologies: A multiline graph tracking cost decreases across 3D printing, solar technology, and genome sequencing, demonstrating how exponential advancement drives exponential cost reduction in emerging technologies. (Bloomberg New Energy Finance & National Human Genome Research Institute, 2023)*

As technologies mature, they become not only more efficient but also more accessible. This democratization of technology drives further innovation and adoption, creating a cycle of progress. The exponential curve of technology, thus, isn't just a pattern of growth but a blueprint for understanding how profound shifts in cost and capability affect everything from global economics to everyday life.

Understanding New Normals in the Quantum Revolution

In the Quantum Era, the traditional models and laws may soon be outdated as we witness technologies like AI advancing themselves. From Anthropic to OpenAI, today's leading AI organizations are developing AI that actually can create other (and better) AI—leading to an explosive growth curve that defies today's "laws." Blockchain technology, despite its slower start, promises to reimagine entire industries. And then, there's quantum computing—putting an end to Moore's Law.

Rose vs. Moore

Moore's Law has long served as a touchstone in understanding the exponential growth of computational power. However, as we approach the physical and practical limits of silicon-based technologies, Rose's Law emerges as a significant disruptor, challenging the foundational expectations set by Moore's Law.

Rose's Law, associated with the advancements in quantum computing developed by Geordie Rose of D-Wave Systems, posits an even more rapid acceleration in computational capabilities than Moore's Law predicts, but in the quantum realm (Rose, 2014). Unlike traditional computing, which relies on bits as the smallest unit of data, quantum computing uses qubits, which can represent and store information in a fundamentally different way thanks to principles like superposition and entanglement. Rose's Law suggests that the power of quantum computers, measured in terms of quantum volume or the number of qubits, is increasing at a pace that could outstrip the biennial doubling anticipated by Moore's Law. This not only represents a quantitative increase in processing power but a qualitative leap in the types of computations that can be performed.

The breaking of old laws marks a new era in which traditional models of technological advancement are being rewritten by the groundbreaking potential of technologies like AI, blockchain, and quantum computing. These technologies are not simply iterations on existing frameworks; they are revolutionary in nature, offering new ways to process, secure, and leverage information at unprecedented scales.

As such, they demand a reevaluation of how we anticipate technological growth and assess its economic and societal impacts. The predictable patterns of the past are giving way to advancement trajectories that are less linear and predictable and more rapid and sporadic. With this in mind, I'd like to introduce you to Amara.

Amara vs. Kurzweil

Ray Kurzweil's optimistic projection posits that each generation of technological evolution occurs at an exponentially faster rate, enhancing our capabilities dramatically and predictably over time. However, Roy Amara, a respected thinker on futures studies, offers a sobering counterpoint. Amara's Law suggests that we tend to overestimate the effect of a technology in the short term and underestimate its effect in the long term (Amara, 1978).

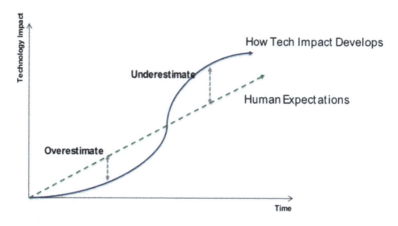

Figure 3-7. *Amara's Law and Technology Hype Cycle: A dual-axis visualization merging Amara's Law with Gartner's Hype Cycle, showing the typical pattern of overestimating technology's short-term impact while underestimating its long-term effects. (Gartner Research & Amara's Original Framework, 2023)*

As it relates to Gartner's Hype Cycle, this principle illuminates why the initial excitement about groundbreaking technologies often leads to inflated expectations, followed by a period of disillusionment when the anticipated breakthroughs do not materialize as quickly or as dramatically as predicted.

- *Reflection on Hype Cycles:* Technologies often undergo a period of hype, followed by disillusionment, before reaching a plateau of productivity. Amara's Law helps explain why the initial excitement might lead to disappointment, yet ultimately, the technology becomes deeply integrated into society.

- *Reevaluation of Capabilities:* For exponential growth technologies like AI, which progresses from simple tasks to more complex and generative capabilities, Amara's Law encourages ongoing reevaluation of what these technologies are capable of achieving as they mature.

- *Enhanced Strategic Decision-Making:* In business and investment, understanding the implications of Amara's Law allows for more strategic decision-making, focusing on potential long-term gains rather than short-lived trends.

It also provides a crucial correction to the linear extrapolation often seen in Kurzweil's predictions, particularly when applied to revolutionary technologies like AI, blockchain, and quantum computing.

With these principles established, we can examine how Amara's Law manifests in today's most transformative technologies. Perhaps nowhere is this pattern more evident than in the field of artificial intelligence, where cycles of enthusiasm and disappointment have played out repeatedly over decades. By analyzing AI's journey through this lens, we can better understand both the limitations of our predictions and the true potential of emerging technologies.

AI and Amara's Influence

Consider AI, which has journeyed through multiple winters and renaissances. Kurzweil's predictions, particularly his anticipation of AI matching human intelligence by 2025, were initially viewed through a lens of boundless optimism. Yet, the reality has been far more tumultuous, with early AI systems struggling to meet the high expectations set during the initial hype. This overestimation in the short run led to disillusionment, even as the long-term potential of AI to transform our lives remains vast and largely untapped.

Short-Term Overestimation:

- *Early Predictions*: In the early days of AI, predictions included the belief that machines would quickly surpass human intelligence. The AI winter, a period of reduced funding and interest in AI research during the 1970s and 1980s, was partly a result of earlier disappointments when the lofty expectations of general AI were not met.

- *Hype Reemergence*: More recently, with the resurgence of AI due to advances in machine learning and deep learning, similar cycles of hype have occurred. Predictions about AI solving all of humanity's problems, or conversely, leading to its downfall, have proliferated.

Long-Term Underestimation:

- *Broader Impacts Emerging*: AI is now driving fundamental changes in multiple sectors, including healthcare, where it assists in diagnosing diseases more accurately and in personalizing treatment plans. In transportation, AI is at the heart of autonomous vehicle technology. In customer service, AI powers chatbots that improve user experience. The depth and breadth of AI's integration into daily life and its potential to reshape entire industries were often underestimated in its earlier phases.

Blockchain's Reality Check

Blockchain technology, heralded as a transformative force for everything from finance to logistics, also aligns with Amara's observation. The initial excitement surrounding blockchain led to speculative bubbles, such as the infamous cryptocurrency boom and bust in 2020 and the NFT frenzy (remember the Bored Ape Project?) around the same time. While Kurzweil might predict a smooth, exponential adoption curve, the reality has been more complex. Blockchain is now slowly finding its footing in practical, albeit less sensational, applications underscoring the underestimated long-term applications that Amara's Law predicts.

Short-Term Overestimation:

- *Initial Hype*: When blockchain technology first emerged, primarily through the rise of Bitcoin, it was heralded as a revolutionary technology that would disrupt financial systems globally, replacing banks and ending the era of centralized financial authority. Initial ICO (Initial Coin Offering) boom led to inflated valuations and speculative investments in numerous blockchain projects.

- *Disillusionment*: Many of these early blockchain projects failed to deliver on their ambitious promises. The technology faced significant challenges including scalability issues, high energy consumption, regulatory hurdles, and slow adoption in mainstream finance. This period reflected a classic "trough of disillusionment," where the technology struggled to meet the overinflated expectations.

Long-Term Underestimation:

- *Gradual Maturation*: Over time, the application of blockchain has extended beyond cryptocurrencies. It is being increasingly integrated into areas such as supply chain management, secure voting systems, real estate for title management, the tokenization of real-world assets, and more. The technology's ability to provide transparency, security, and decentralization is beginning to transform these industries in profound ways, suggesting that the long-term impact of blockchain is likely still underappreciated.

Quantum Computing's Slow Burn

Quantum computing, perhaps the quintessential example of Amara's Law in action, continues to challenge Kurzweil's accelerated timelines. Despite significant theoretical advancements, practical quantum computing remains in its nascent stages, with real-world applications yet to be realized. The field's complexity and the technical challenges of maintaining quantum states mean that its short-term impact has been less than many predicted. However, the potential for quantum computing in the future cannot be overstated.

Short-Term Overestimation:

- *Early Predictions*: Initially, quantum computing was celebrated as the next major leap in computational power, expected to solve complex problems within minutes that would take traditional computers millennia to solve. Enthusiasm led to bold claims about near-term impacts on drug discovery, cryptography, and other fields.

- *Hype Reemergence*: As companies like Google and IBM began to unveil their first quantum processors, media and industry hype suggested that quantum supremacy—the point at which quantum computers can perform tasks beyond the reach of classical computers—was imminent. This hype often glossed over the immense technical challenges still to be addressed.

Long-Term Underestimation:

- *Broader Impacts Emerging*: Despite the slow progress in overcoming quantum computing's initial obstacles, its potential applications continue to expand. In finance, quantum algorithms could one day optimize portfolios and model financial markets with unprecedented complexity. In logistics, they might solve large-scale optimization problems that are currently infeasible. The integration of quantum computing into practical applications is more gradual and less sensational than early predictions suggested, yet its potential to revolutionize data security, materials science, and complex system modeling could far exceed initial forecasts.

This pattern is not new. The development of major technologies, from the steam engine to electricity, has often followed a similar path of initial overestimation followed by transformative long-term impact. Each of these technologies experienced periods of hype, followed by disillusionment, and ultimately, integration into the fabric of society in ways that were initially difficult to predict. Ultimately, the predictability of the unpredictable (nonlinear) growth of groundbreaking technologies lies in the macrofactors that either prohibit or enable its advancement. As described earlier in the book, regardless of what "law" you ascribe to, one can only understand a technology's trajectory (and ultimate success or failure in the short and long term) by fully grasping the force field factors at play.

Force Field Factors at Play

The "force field factors"—a synergy of societal, governmental, economic, and infrastructural conditions—must align for exponential growth. These factors must be aligned for a technology to transcend from a novel idea to a ubiquitous tool.

Consider the streaming revolution—a paradigm not merely accelerated by the advent of high-speed Internet but propelled by a society increasingly disposed to on-demand consumption, supportive policies that encouraged digital markets, and the infrastructure that enabled seamless, instant access to vast libraries of content.

In contrast, quantum computing, despite its potential, is currently hindered by high costs and a lack of user-friendly software. AR/VR has struggled with user adoption due to the clunkiness of hardware and a lack of compelling content, reflecting the absence of conducive force field factors. (See Chapter 1 for more details on force field factors.)

Understanding Scaling

The "force field factors" are indeed crucial for the gestation and ongoing momentum of a technology, but for that momentum to be sustained, to truly penetrate the fabric of society, scaling is imperative. While the hype cycle describes the emotional and speculative journey of a technology, scaling represents the practical and operational expansion of that technology across markets and sectors. It is the process by which a technology increases in scope and utility, becoming not just available but integral. Scaling is where potential meets practicality.

As we scrutinize the trajectories of burgeoning technologies like quantum computing and augmented reality, we must recognize that without effective scaling strategies, their impact will remain limited. Therefore, understanding and investing in the scaling of a technology is as critical as aligning the force field factors that allow it to take root. It is at this intersection of potential and practicality that the future of any technology is truly decided.

Scaling and Hype Cycles:

- Scaling is significantly influenced by the hype cycle a technology undergoes. During the Peak of Inflated Expectations, technologies might see a surge in interest and premature scaling attempts, which might not be sustainable.

- As the technology enters the Trough of Disillusionment, scaling efforts may stall as stakeholders become skeptical of the technology's practical value and implementation difficulties become apparent.

- The Slope of Enlightenment and the Plateau of Productivity are crucial for sustainable scaling, as the technology's applications, strengths, and limitations become clearer. Here, technology adoption becomes more strategic, and true scaling begins as more sectors integrate the technology into everyday operations.

Scaling is the crucible in which a technology's resilience and adaptability are tested, a necessary phase that propels an innovation from novelty to norm. But beyond the singular journey of scaling, there is an even more profound phenomenon: the "convergence effect." It's here, at the confluence of revolutionary technologies, where the sum becomes greater than its parts. As different technological pathways merge—AI with quantum computing or blockchain with the Internet of Things—their individual impacts don't just add up, they synergize. This convergence creates an ecosystem of interlocking advancements, fostering new capabilities and applications that redefine what technology can achieve and accelerating our leap into a future brimming with uncharted potential.

Convergence: Compounding Exponential Growth

The power of convergence lies in the compounded impact where technologies interlace to amplify each other's strengths and diminish their individual weaknesses.

When it comes to today's most transformational technologies, the "convergence effect" is truly revolutionary. AI brings the power of prediction, adaptation, and automation. Blockchain introduces an immutable ledger, transparency, and security. Quantum computing offers computational leaps that defy conventional limits. Separately, each represents a significant stride forward; together, they are unstoppable—leading us toward an era of innovation that is bound to reshape the world as we know it. This is not just additive; it's multiplicative. The convergence of these technologies means smarter systems, more secure and efficient operations, and solutions to problems we haven't even identified yet.

But it's not just these three technologies that are converging. The Quantum Revolution is also seeing IoT, genomics, and other innovations work together to eventually create a singular, seamless experience.

When transformational technologies intertwine, their combined force field factors can compound, creating unprecedented acceleration. As an example, the integration of IoT, AI, and blockchain could usher in a new era of smart cities, where urban environments respond in real time to various stimuli, optimizing everything from traffic to energy use:

- *Traffic Management:* IoT devices can monitor traffic in real time, collecting data on vehicle flows, pedestrian numbers, and even weather conditions. AI can analyze this data to predict traffic jams before they occur and adjust signals accordingly to optimize flow. Meanwhile, blockchain can securely store this data, ensuring that all adjustments to traffic signals and data exchanges between devices are transparent and immutable.

- *Energy Management:* In smart grids, IoT devices can track energy usage across different parts of the city in real time. AI can then optimize energy distribution based on immediate demand and predict future needs. Blockchain technology can be used to create a decentralized record of energy transactions, facilitating the use of microgrids and the exchange of energy between consumers, which can stabilize demand and supply.

Technology convergence is particularly promising for medicine and enhanced patient care. Imagine a scenario where a patient with a chronic condition such as heart disease wears a smartwatch that monitors their heart activity, physical activity, and other vital signs. IoT devices transmit this data securely through a blockchain network, ensuring it remains private and tamper-proof. AI algorithms analyze this data to detect early signs of a potential heart attack or other health deterioration, alerting healthcare providers and the patient with recommendations for preventive measures or immediate actions. This could include suggesting medication adjustments or scheduling an urgent doctor's visit.

This integrative approach exemplifies how, across various sectors, the convergence of technologies is not just enhancing existing frameworks but revolutionizing them, promising better outcomes through smarter, more connected, and secure systems.

Taking Advantage of Exponential Moments

As Stephen McBride, Chief Analyst at RiskHedge, recently stated, "We've been stuck in a mini 'dark age' for disruption over the past 15 years. New innovations were mostly 'meh'. Snagging dates on Tinder… uploading photos to Instagram… ordering pizzas through DoorDash (DASH)… and watching Netflix (NFLX) are cool, but shallow. They didn't push humanity forward like jet engines, refrigeration, or indoor plumbing did. The good news: We're entering a new golden age of disruption."

This "golden age" (a.k.a. Quantum Revolution) is being driven by AI, blockchain, and quantum computing, and investors find themselves at the starting blocks of potentially the greatest wealth creation opportunity of their lifetimes. However, this is not your run-of-the-mill investment landscape. It's complex, fast-evolving, and fraught with as much potential for spectacular failures as it is for historic gains.

Recognizing exponential technologies is inherently challenging; our brains are wired to anticipate linear progressions, making it difficult to track the steep ascent of exponential curves. This cognitive bias often leads us to underestimate the pace at which emerging technologies mature, only recognizing their exponential nature when it's already too late.

That's why investors navigating the swiftly evolving landscape need to integrate multiple perspectives into their decision-making process to capitalize on emerging opportunities effectively. A deep understanding of exponential growth and compressed innovation cycles is essential. Technology can evolve and reach maturity much quicker than in the past, which means the window for investment and action can be surprisingly short, and once growth kicks in, it can be staggeringly rapid. Technologies that may initially appear nascent could achieve market saturation within just a few years.

Simultaneously, investors must meticulously analyze the "force field factors"—societal, economic, governmental, and infrastructural elements that must align for a technology to truly flourish. This involves a thorough assessment of the regulatory environment, market readiness, societal trends, and the available infrastructure, all of which can significantly impact a technology's adoption and success.

Moreover, the convergence of multiple technologies can catalyze new applications and markets, creating exponential value. Investors should be on the lookout for opportunities where technologies like AI, blockchain, and IoT intersect, as these can lead to innovative solutions that redefine industries. Understanding how these technologies complement and enhance each other can uncover hidden opportunities and allow investors to be part of defining the future.

Lastly, a critical skill for investors in this era is the ability to identify inflection points—key moments when a technology shifts from an experimental phase to broader acceptance or when a breakthrough resolves a significant limitation. Recognizing these inflection points is crucial as they often precede rapid market expansion and can be the optimal times for making strategic investment decisions. This holistic approach goes well beyond financial acumen and even luck. It requires foresight and a profound understanding of technological trajectories, the state of the world around us, and potential tipping points that take something from "meh" to "WOW!"

Summary

Here's what's fascinating about exponential growth in technology: it's not just about the pace of change—it's about how that pace is fundamentally reshaping the relationship between human perception and technological reality. We're living through a moment where our inherited mental models for understanding progress have become obsolete faster than we've been able to update them.

Every time we believe we've grasped how quickly things are changing, we're probably still thinking too linearly. The rules that governed technological advancement for decades—Moore's Law, Metcalfe's Law—are being superseded by something more complex and interconnected. When quantum computing meets AI meets blockchain, we're not just adding these technologies together; we're creating entirely new possibilities that we couldn't have predicted by looking at each innovation in isolation.

Success in this era isn't about predicting specific technological outcomes—it's about developing frameworks that can adapt to exponential change happening in real time. For investors, business leaders, and really all of us, this means learning to think differently about time itself. What once took decades now takes months, and by the time something becomes obvious, the real opportunity has usually passed.

That's what makes this moment so critical. We're not just witnessing the acceleration of technology; we're being forced to accelerate our own capacity to understand and respond to change. And that might be the most important adaptation of all.

CHAPTER 4

Inflection Points and the Difference Between Reality and Hype

Back in the early 1990s, while the rest of the credit card industry was still a "one-size-fits-all" industry mostly relying on gut feelings and personal judgment to determine whether or not someone "deserved" credit, I was at Capital One, a company that was betting big on something totally different. Capital One's founders, Rich Fairbank and Nigel Morris, saw the chaos, the inefficiency, and smelled opportunity. Why? Because credit decisions, a domain traditionally governed by human whims, were ripe for disruption.

This disruption wasn't just about swapping out humans for algorithms. Rather, it was about fundamentally reinventing the profitability model of credit cards. Our master plan? Leverage data in a way that had never been done before in this sector—turn those numbers into a goldmine by segmenting the population; customizing products, services, and operations to these segments; and automating decision-making using robust, statistically proven, and revalidated models.

© Tal Elyashiv 2025
T. Elyashiv, *Investing in Revolutions*, https://doi.org/10.1007/979-8-8688-1177-7_4

We weren't just throwing tech at a problem and hoping for the best. It was about rigorously testing, tweaking, and validating these models to ensure they not only worked but outperformed any traditional method out there. We dove deep into consumer behavior, scientifically tested various hypotheses, adjusted our algorithms, and iterated relentlessly. Because we knew that consumer behavior isn't static; it's as dynamic as the New York stock exchange—always fluctuating, always evolving. Our models had to be just as agile.

After a couple of years of perfecting our model for rethinking the credit card ecosystem, the internal metrics were shocking (in the best sense of the word). By the late 1990s, it became crystal clear: our data-driven approach was not only profitable; it was revolutionary. The result? Capital One became one of the largest issuers of credit cards in the United States and turned the entire industry on its head (Capital One Annual Report, 1994).

That's the thing about inflection points—you don't just find them; sometimes you forge them yourself.

The Essence of Inflection Points

An inflection point represents a pivotal moment that dramatically reshapes the trajectory of a technology, industry, or even the global economy. These are the junctures at which the future becomes rewritten, where new opportunities emerge, often with profound economic and cultural implications.

The funny thing about inflection points is that they can only be identified in retrospect. Predicting an inflection point before it becomes one is near impossible, but there are smoke signals that if one is looking for signs, it can indicate something very big is coming.

Entrepreneur and author, Eric Sinoway, pointed out that "Inflection points come in all forms: positive, negative, easy, hard, obvious, and subtle. The way you respond – whether you grab hold of an inflection point and leverage it for all it's worth or just let it carry you along – is as important as the event itself."

These moments could emerge from the euphoria of technological breakthroughs or be born from the ashes of social upheaval and disaster. They're pivotal, rare, and profoundly transformative, marking a before and an after in society.

Think of inflection points as the intersection where forces of change—be they technological innovation or societal shifts—collide with the momentum of the moment to forge a path that's radically different from anything that's come before. Whether sparked by inspiration or desperation, these are the points that rewrite our future, setting the stage for a new set of rules, a new way of life.

Technological Inflection Points

A technology inflection point is a moment when a technology goes from being a niche interest to an absolute necessity, practically overnight. This is the point where the growth curve isn't just climbing; it's going vertical. These are the innovations that have reshaped communication, commerce, and global connectivity, and are the catalysts that render old systems obsolete and spawn entirely new industries.

- *The iPhone Launch (2007):* Steve Jobs unveiling the iPhone in January 2007 was not just a product announcement; it was a cultural phenomenon. He famously said, "Today, Apple is going to reinvent the phone," and he wasn't exaggerating. The iPhone combined a phone, an iPod, and an Internet communicator into one device, fundamentally changing the smartphone market and consumer expectations around mobile technology.

- *IBM's Deep Blue Beats Kasparov (1997):* When IBM's Deep Blue defeated world chess champion Garry Kasparov in 1997, it was a watershed moment for artificial intelligence. This event publicly demonstrated AI's potential to outperform human intelligence in specific tasks, sparking interest and investment in AI research that continues to shape the field.

- *The Launch of Windows 95 (1995):* Windows 95's release was not just significant for Microsoft; it marked a pivotal moment in personal computing. Its launch event featured the Rolling Stones' "Start Me Up," a fitting anthem for a product that would kickstart widespread adoption of GUI-based operating systems and fundamentally change how people interacted with computers.

Economic Inflection Points

An economic inflection point fundamentally alters the business landscape due to technological breakthroughs, significant policy changes, market crashes, or radical shifts in consumer preferences. Each of these can trigger waves of effects across the global economy, sparking new opportunities and, yes, often creating substantial risks.

- *The Great Depression (1929):* This catastrophic economic downturn marked one of the most significant inflection points in modern history. Beginning with the stock market crash in 1929, it led to a decade of economic hardship worldwide. This period reshaped US and global economic policies, leading to significant government interventions in the economy, including the New Deal in the United States.

- *Bretton Woods Agreement (1944):* At the end of World War II, the Bretton Woods Conference established the US dollar as the backbone of international exchange, setting fixed currency rates to the dollar and tying the dollar to gold. This agreement laid the foundation for the postwar global economic order and led to the creation of key international financial institutions like the International Monetary Fund (IMF) and the World Bank.

- *The Oil Crises of the 1970s:* The oil crises of 1973 and 1979, when oil prices spiked due to geopolitical tensions in the Middle East, served as significant economic inflection points. They triggered stagflation in many developed economies, combining high unemployment and inflation, which led to a shift in energy policies, greater exploration of alternative energy sources, and changes in consumer behavior regarding energy consumption.

- *The Financial Crisis of 2008:* Triggered by the collapse of the housing market in the United States due to subprime mortgage defaults, this crisis led to a severe global economic recession. It brought about major regulatory reforms in financial sectors worldwide and led to significant shifts in consumer trust and banking practices.

Economic shifts can be equally transformative. For businesses and investors, such moments underscore the importance of vigilance—of keeping an eye on economic trends that could signal a downturn or an opportunity. It's about more than survival; it's about understanding that within economic upheaval lies the potential for innovation and the emergence of new markets.

Sociopolitical Inflection Points

Then, there are the sociopolitical shifts, where legislation, policy changes, or even shifts in political stability can pivot the market or a whole society. Several force field factors can converge to create a sociopolitical inflection point, and understanding these can help in anticipating potential shifts or in navigating them once they occur. Here are some of the primary contributors:

- *Social Movements:* Grassroots movements driven by collective action can reach a tipping point that challenges and ultimately changes existing power structures or norms. The Civil Rights Movement in the 1960s in the United States, for instance, led to major legislative changes regarding racial equality.

- *Economic Disparities:* Economic crises or growing inequality can spur significant sociopolitical changes. For example, the Labor Wars in the early twentieth century was marked by a profound transformation in the labor landscape, largely fueled by stark economic disparities and rapid industrialization. As the wealth generated by industrial expansion was not equitably distributed, the glaring disparity between the burgeoning industrial moguls and the struggling working class became increasingly untenable. Public outrage catalyzed significant labor reforms, leading to the establishment of the Department of Labor and the passage of the Clayton Antitrust Act, which recognized the legality of labor unions and aimed to improve the bargaining power of workers.

- *Technological Advances:* New technologies that reshape communication, work, or life can also precipitate sociopolitical changes. The advent of the Internet and social media has altered political campaigns, movements, and the very nature of public discourse. Take the Arab Spring in late 2010, which marked a profound moment in the political landscape of the Arab world, with a wave of protests, uprisings, and armed rebellions sweeping across numerous countries. A defining feature of these movements was their adept use of social media to organize, communicate, and amplify their cause, showcasing the formidable role of digital tools in challenging deep-seated political structures.

- *Political Leadership Changes:* The rise or fall of transformative political leaders can serve as inflection points. Leadership changes can alter a country's direction through new policies or ideologies, as seen with Franklin D. Roosevelt's New Deal or more recently with the global shift toward populist leaders.

- *Ideological Shifts:* Significant changes in the dominant societal values or beliefs, often driven by generational shifts, intellectual movements, or reactions to current events, can lead to sociopolitical inflection points. The shift toward more liberal attitudes on issues like marriage equality over the past decades is an example of such a shift.

- *Global Influences:* In an interconnected world, events in one country can trigger sociopolitical changes globally. The fall of the Soviet Union, for instance, not only reshaped global politics but also had deep impacts on national policies and political ideologies around the world. The Fall of the Berlin Wall symbolized the end of the Cold War and led to the reunification of Germany and the broader integration of Eastern Europe into the global capitalist economy. It opened up new markets and led to significant economic reforms and investments in the region.

- *External Shocks:* Events such as wars, pandemics, or natural disasters can drastically alter political and social landscapes, often accelerating or redirecting existing trends. The COVID-19 pandemic, for example, wasn't just a health crisis; it was a cataclysm that thrust technology deep into the fabric of everyday life, reshaping the workforce and redrawing the boundaries of societal norms. This period, which is still very much ongoing, turbocharged technological adoption and innovation, pulling the future into the present whether people wanted it or not.

In the throes of the pandemic, we witnessed a decade's worth of digital transformation crammed into mere months. According to McKinsey & Company (2020), companies accelerated their digital transformation by an average of seven years during the first eight months of the pandemic. Lockdowns mandated a massive pivot to remote work, elevating platforms like Zoom, Microsoft Teams, and Slack from handy tools to the backbone of our economic engine. But beyond the tools, the entire approach to work—hundreds of years of workplace norms—was turned upside down.

And then, there's the societal shake-up. The digital divide, once a theoretical debate for many, became starkly visible, as access to reliable Internet suddenly dictated who could work or learn and who was left behind. This drove fresh investments in digital infrastructure and a rethinking of Internet access as essential infrastructure, akin to water or electricity.

In essence, COVID-19 wasn't just a disruptor—it was the mother of reinvention, forcing technology into even tighter integration with our daily lives. It reshaped norms, tested the resilience of our infrastructure, and sped up a wave of digital transformation that will mold our existence for years to come.

Inflection Point Aftershocks

Aftershock inflection points are those that follow in the steps of a first order inflection point to create multiple reverberations of value. Aftershocks arise when an initial inflection point expands beyond its original domain, catalyzing new opportunities and applications. These second-order creations can sometimes surpass the impact of the original innovation, expanding its utility and reshaping additional sectors in unforeseen ways. This pattern is evident throughout the history of technology, where the primary breakthrough sets the stage, but it is the subsequent adaptations and innovations that fully realize and sometimes expand the technology's transformative potential.

Just as an earthquake represents a profound shift in the earth's structure, a technology inflection point marks a radical change in the technological landscape. It's the moment when a new technology or innovation disrupts existing markets, obliterates old paradigms, and creates new opportunities. Like the sudden release of stress along a geological fault line, these technology shifts can happen abruptly and often unexpectedly, reconfiguring the industry landscape in profound ways.

Following the initial quake, aftershocks are inevitable. In geological terms, these are smaller quakes that occur as the earth's crust adjusts to the equilibrium disrupted by the initial seismic event. In technology, these aftershocks are the subsequent innovations triggered by the primary inflection point. They may be less dramatic, but their cumulative effects can be just as profound, if not more so, than the initial breakthrough.

Take, for example, the smartphone revolution initiated by the iPhone. If the launch of the iPhone was the earthquake, the aftershocks have been the myriad developments that followed: app ecosystems, mobile banking, real-time navigation, and augmented reality, each spawning their own minirevolutions in personal computing, finance, transportation, and media.

The Most Valuable Companies Capitalize on Multiple Inflection Points

They all created or benefited from a first inflection point and have taken advantage of following inflection points, while investing R&D ahead of possible future inflection points.

Company	First Inflection Point	Expansion Enabled by Select Inflection Points	Possible Future Inflection Points
Apple	Personal Computer	Internet Broadband Mobile	4G AR/VR AVs
Microsoft	Personal Computer	Internet Broadband Cloud Computing	AI/ML AR/VR Quantum Computing
amazon	Internet	Broadband Cloud Computing Robotics	AVs AI/ML
Alphabet	Internet	Broadband Mobile Cloud Computing	AI/ML AVs Quantum Computing
FACEBOOK	Internet	Broadband Mobile AI/ML	AR/VR Telecom

a mhdempsey

Figure 4-1. Technology Aftershocks from Primary Innovations Introduction: This visualization demonstrates how primary technological breakthroughs create cascading effects across multiple sectors and applications. Using the example of the iPhone's introduction, it maps out the subsequent innovations and industry transformations that followed the initial breakthrough. (Morgan Stanley Research, 2023)

The aftershock moments spurred by AI and blockchain are brimming with potential yet are shrouded in uncertainty. How will AI's advancement in natural language processing transform education and access to information globally? What new business models will blockchain enable?

The challenge now is to harness these technologies responsibly while preparing for their broad societal impacts. As these aftershocks continue to reverberate, they will inevitably give rise to new ethical dilemmas, regulatory challenges, and shifts in socio-economic structures. Navigating this landscape will require foresight, adaptability, and a nuanced understanding of technology's dual-edged potential to transform and disrupt.

Distinguishing Hype from Inflection Points

Hype is that loud, seductive siren call that surrounds new technologies and ideas, blasting from every media outlet with promises of revolutionizing the market or consumer behavior. But let's cut through that noise: hype doesn't always mean impact. It's a frothy excitement that can pump up expectations to levels that reality can't possibly match, leading often to a bubble that bursts just as spectacularly as it formed.

Hype can sometimes reflect genuine excitement and potential around new technologies, but it does not always guarantee their practical impact or viability. It can amplify expectations to unrealistic levels, leading to inevitable disappointments. The challenge for investors is to distinguish between the two. This isn't about just being skeptical; it's about being strategic—leveraging foresight and a deep understanding of the force field factors surrounding whatever new tech comes our way.

Take the dot-com bubble of the late 1990s and early 2000s, which was a period characterized by excessive hype around Internet companies. Many investments were made on the basis of potential rather than proven business models, leading to a market crash. However, those that survived, like Amazon and Google, adjusted and continued to thrive, underscoring the importance of discerning sustainable business models in the midst of hype.

And then, there are more recent examples of feverishly hyped up technology that got their 15 seconds of fame but eventually landed in the "Trough of Disillusionment" never to recover.

Google Glass

Introduced in 2012, Google Glass was expected to pioneer widespread adoption of augmented reality (AR). The pitch was compelling: information floating right before your eyes, seamlessly integrating with your daily life. Yet, it quickly became apparent that society wasn't ready to embrace this sci-fi accessory. Privacy nightmares, the awkwardness of public use, and a lack of compelling applications turned Glass from a must-have into a pariah, worn by few beyond the "Glassholes" who dared to don them in social settings. It's a textbook case of how even the most cutting-edge technology can stumble if it ignores the societal and ethical landscapes it seeks to inhabit.

Theranos

Then, there's Theranos, which became the darling of Silicon Valley not through proven results but through a narrative so compelling that it blinded many to the truth. Promising to revolutionize healthcare with a device that could run myriad tests on just a few drops of blood, Theranos attracted millions in investment and significant public interest. However, the reality was a stark contrast: the technology was fundamentally flawed, and the company's unethical maneuvers to hide these shortcomings led to one of the most dramatic downfalls in the tech and healthcare industries. Theranos didn't just fail to deliver; it actively deceived, showcasing how hype can mask a dangerous absence of substance and ethical rigor.

Foresight: The Antidote to Hype

First appearing in Chapter 2, foresight is an ongoing theme (and a skill) because of its importance in navigating various aspects of technology revolutions—especially when evaluating the sometimes blurred line between true inflection points and mere hype. The challenge lies in discerning genuine opportunities from the cacophony of overhyped fads. This discernment is critical not merely for the investor looking to allocate capital wisely but for anyone seeking to understand where our society might be heading next.

To effectively separate the wheat from the chaff, one cannot simply ride the wave of popular sentiment. To truly discern what's transformative from what's transient, one must dive deep. This means not only keeping abreast of technological advancements but also understanding the broader context in which these innovations operate—the force field factors. Unlike hype, which can flourish without these factors fully aligning, true inflection points depend on them.

Inflection point foresight involves scrutinizing the ecosystem surrounding a technology. Are regulators keeping pace? Is the market ready or resistant? What cultural shifts might accelerate or impede adoption? These questions are fundamental. By integrating diverse perspectives and applying a critical lens to the prevailing narrative, one can sift through the sensational to find the substantive.

Hype As an Indicator, Not a Verdict

It's crucial to recognize that while hype is not always rooted in current reality, it does serve as an indicator that something significant may be on the horizon. Hype can be a version of smoke signals, but as usual, there's always more to the story. For example, the initial excitement around blockchain in 2017 and 2018 did not immediately result in widespread practical applications.

Blockchain's Inflection Point

Blockchain technology has had its narrative sometimes overshadowed by the frenzy around cryptocurrencies and NFTs. While these applications have introduced blockchain to a broader audience, they have also led to speculative bubbles, characterized by extreme price volatility and questionable long-term value. The real transformative power of blockchain, however, is evidenced in more substantial initiatives driven by large corporations like Alphabet, Samsung, and Microsoft, as well as many top financial industry players like JP Morgan, Morgan Stanley, and BlackRock. In fact, one could consider BlackRock's unveiling of the BUIDL fund (BlackRock Investment Report, 2023), which was a strategic investment in the underlying technology of blockchain and its ability to create a more transparent, efficient, and secure framework for conducting global business. This development was a major turning point in traditional finance's integration of blockchain technology into our economic fabric, distinguishing it from the ephemeral hype of quick-profit crypto schemes.

Another aspect of the blockchain ecosystem that may seem like only hype but could be an indicator of things to come is the Metaverse. The Metaverse, built on top of blockchain technology, was supposed to be the next Internet, a virtual landscape where we would socialize, work, and play. But as it turns out, creating a universe is a bit more complicated than just declaring it exists. The technology—clunky VR headsets and still-nascent software ecosystems—hasn't caught up with the ambition...yet. While the public seemed to not fully embrace the most extreme virtual worlds of the Metaverse, it's very clear that it continues to play an increasing role in our everyday lives. That's because the Metaverse is not a video game. The full realization of its value lies in a vision of digital connectivity.

Take the workplace environment. Hopping on a Zoom or WebEx call is second nature to us now. The Metaverse can take that to the next level and create sophisticated virtual work environments that replicate the dynamics of physical offices, allowing for more nuanced and engaging remote work experiences. These virtual spaces can enhance collaboration among global teams, offering tools that support real-time sharing, complex 3D modeling, and immersive presentations that surpass the capabilities of current video conferencing tools. Companies can also leverage the Metaverse for training programs, providing employees with immersive, hands-on learning experiences that are both cost-effective and scalable. For instance, virtual reality simulations can train workers in high-risk industries (like oil rigs, chemical plants, or high-voltage environments) without the associated physical dangers.

Beyond meetings and training at work, the Metaverse could facilitate more accessible healthcare services, allowing patients to visit doctors virtually in a more interactive manner than traditional telemedicine. This could be particularly transformative for patients in remote or underserved regions, improving access to specialists and advanced healthcare services.

So, while Meta's premature version of the Metaverse was a flop, the true purpose and usefulness of the Metaverse is still to come. This isn't about escaping reality; it's about expanding it, blending the digital and physical until the boundaries start to blur. If developers can move beyond the hype and genuinely innovate, we might find ourselves on the cusp of a new digital revolution that reshapes how we interact with the world and each other.

AI's Inflection Point

AI's journey has been marked by cycles of exaggerated expectations followed by disillusionment, only to rise again on the back of genuine advancements. The release of ChatGPT by OpenAI represents an authentic inflection point in AI's history, showcasing a leap from theoretical models to practical, impactful applications. ChatGPT and similar models are not merely incremental improvements but are fundamental shifts in how machines understand and generate human language. This development has spurred a new wave of innovations, with companies and developers leveraging these large language models (LLMs) to create applications that range from improving customer service bots to aiding in complex legal and medical research.

One example of AI's swift and sweeping impact is in software development. Software developers were some of the most sought-after experts by organizations in every industry. However, after the introduction of ChatGPT (AI's inflection point), AI-driven code generators and assistants have become more sophisticated, enabling programmers to streamline their workflow and, in some cases, replace them altogether. These tools can suggest code, help debug, and even write significant portions of code, making the development process faster and more accessible to people with limited coding expertise. And this is just one small example of the extraordinary impact AI is already having on the global economy and the global workforce

Nearly 40% of worldwide employment could be influenced by AI technologies, according to a comprehensive 2024 study by the International Monetary Fund (Georgieva et al., 2024). While this doesn't mean direct job displacement, it does mean that the way we work, interact, think, and communicate will be irrevocably altered in ways we're just now beginning to understand.

Quantum's Inflection Point

Quantum computing promises to revolutionize industries by performing calculations at speeds unattainable by classical computers. The concept hinges on quantum bits, or qubits, which unlike traditional bits that represent data as 0s or 1s can represent both at the same time due to quantum superposition (Preskill, 2012).

However, the journey from theoretical potential to practical application is fraught with technical hurdles. Qubits are highly sensitive to their environment; maintaining their quantum state requires extremely low temperatures and sophisticated error correction methods, which makes building a scalable quantum computer exceptionally challenging. Despite these obstacles, progress is undeniable.

In 2019, Google claimed quantum supremacy (Arute et al., Nature, 2019), successfully performing a test computation in just 200 seconds, which they estimated would have taken the world's most powerful supercomputer 10,000 years to complete. This was a quantum inflection point, or dare I say, "quantum leap."

This particular inflection point wasn't just about speed; it was about the potential to tackle problems that were previously seen as unsolvable. It invited us to reconsider everything from drug development, which could be revolutionized by the ability to model complex molecules more effectively, to climate change, where quantum computing could optimize large systems like electrical grids more efficiently.

As quantum computing progresses, it will likely catalyze a series of "aftershocks" in various domains, reshaping industries and perhaps even the fabric of society in unforeseen ways. It's a thrilling, if uncertain, prospect, challenging us to think differently about technology's role in addressing some of the world's most pressing issues.

Summary

In the opening chapter of this book, the case was made that we're living through one of the most significant transformational periods in history—the close of one revolution and the birth of a new. That, in and of itself, marks a sweeping inflection point.

The pillar technologies of the Quantum Revolution (blockchain, AI, and quantum computing, among others like DNA sequencing and autonomous robotics) are poised to recalibrate everything from market dynamics to societal norms, from how we safeguard our data to how we cultivate our crops. However, this panoptic inflection point is unique.

It marks the transition from digital experience to a world where the digital and physical seamlessly merge, creating a world vastly different from our own.

What defines this inflection point isn't just the technologies themselves but their capacity to redraw the realms of the possible. Our challenge—and it's a mammoth one—is to steer these technologies toward outcomes that uplift rather than unsettle, that democratize rather than divide. The inflection point of the Quantum Revolution is the Big Bang; however, the convergence of these technologies is the force that will shape the cosmos.

CHAPTER 5

The Convergence Effect

Some of us just happen to be fans of the classic 1980s animated television series *Voltron*, which was based on the Japanese anime *Beast King GoLion* and followed the story of five space explorers who pilot giant lion robots. If that wasn't unbelievable enough, these lions could combine to form Voltron, a gigantic robot warrior equipped with a sword and other weapons used to combat evil. Voltron was so much greater than the sum of its feline parts. The merging of each of the lions transcended individual capabilities to transform into a super-being that was more powerful and effective than anything else around it—even its ferocious foes.

Exactly 40 years after the release of its debut episode, we can learn some lessons from Voltron as we explore today's phenomenon of technology convergence.

Just as the lions combined to create a completely new and infinitely more powerful force, the technologies of the Quantum Revolution, while immensely powerful on their own, are and will continue to converge to create a vast ecosystem of new and profoundly more capable platforms than those that exist today. That's because the concept of technology convergence isn't just a subplot; it's a central theme that radically alters the storyline of how we interact with technology. The merging of distinct technologies into a unified system isn't just about technologies working

© Tal Elyashiv 2025
T. Elyashiv, *Investing in Revolutions*, https://doi.org/10.1007/979-8-8688-1177-7_5

together to merely add to our toolkit; it multiplexes capabilities, creates entirely new platforms for interaction, and will redefine our own societal norms and economic landscapes.

Technology convergence has a profound ability to reshape consumption and usage patterns, enabling use cases that were previously impractical or unimaginable. When technologies merge, they don't just stack; they synthesize and catalyze further technological adoption. This synthesis results in impacts that ripple across multiple industries, transforming them in fundamental ways.

Consider the fusion of social media and mobile technology. This convergence didn't merely change how we communicate; it revolutionized how we consume information and perceive the world. Mobile social media has accelerated the spread of information (and misinformation), broadened our social networks beyond geographical limits, and even reshaped political landscapes. It's a stark illustration of how technological convergence can amplify the social impact of each component technology.

However, the story of convergence is not solely one of creation but also of obsolescence. As new converged technologies emerge, they frequently render existing products and markets irrelevant. The smartphone is a prime example—it absorbed and surpassed the functionalities of music players, video players, cameras, and GPS devices. Each capability it integrated led to the decline of standalone products that once seemed indispensable. Similarly, the rise of streaming services, bolstered by the convergence of broadband Internet and mobile technology, has not only decimated the CD and DVD industries but has also severely challenged traditional movie theaters and cable television.

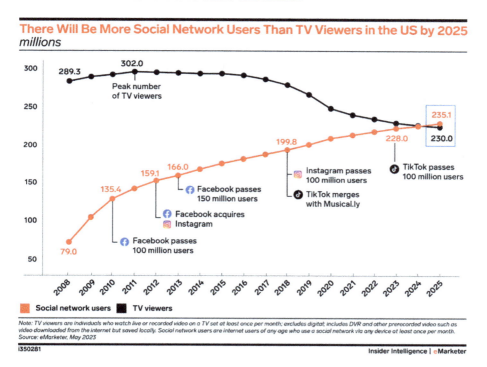

Figure 5-1. *Technology Convergence Impact Model Introduction: This visualization demonstrates how different technologies merge to create new capabilities and obsolete older systems, particularly highlighting the smartphone's role in displacing standalone devices. Source: Harvard Business Review, 2023*

The implications of these shifts are profound. On one hand, they democratize access to technology, making powerful tools available right in one's pocket. On the other, they can lead to significant disruptions in job markets, necessitate shifts in regulatory landscapes, and demand new strategies from existing businesses.

Convergence isn't just an additive factor in technology growth—it's an exponential one. It has the power to rapidly accelerate the adoption of new technologies while simultaneously phasing out the old. This Voltronic force of creation and destruction is a critical consideration for anyone involved in technological development, investment, or policymaking.

Understanding the dynamics at play is crucial for navigating the challenges and opportunities that lie ahead. For policymakers, entrepreneurs, and investors alike, recognizing the potential of technology convergence will be key to adapting and thriving in a dynamic digital landscape.

The Quantum Revolution's Voltron

Stated in ARK Invest's Big Ideas 2024 Report, "convergence among disruptive technologies will define this decade (ARK Invest, 2024). Five major technology platforms—Artificial Intelligence, Blockchain, Multi Omic Sequencing, Energy Storage, and Robotics—are coalescing and should transform global economic activity. Technological convergence could create tectonic macroeconomic shifts more impactful than the first and second industrial revolutions."

The report goes on to say that "Globally, real economic growth could accelerate from 3% on average during the past 125 years to more than 7% during the next 7 years as robots reinvigorate manufacturing, robotaxis transform transportation, and artificial intelligence amplifies knowledge worker productivity. Catalyzed by breakthroughs in artificial intelligence, the global equity market value associated with disruptive innovation could increase from 16% of the total* to more than 60% by 2030. As a result, the annualized equity return associated with disruptive innovation could exceed 40% during the next seven years, increasing its market capitalization from ~$19 trillion today to roughly $220 trillion by 2030."

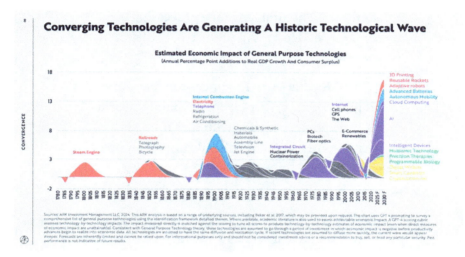

Figure 5-2. *Projected Market Value of Disruptive Technologies Introduction: This graph illustrates the anticipated growth in market capitalization of disruptive technologies from current levels to 2030, based on ARK Invest's analysis. Source: ARK Invest Big Ideas Report (2024)*

To understand how quickly these disruptive technologies are progressing (and converging), PwC recently had to update its 2016 evaluation of critical technologies reshaping how we live, work, and conduct business. AI, AR, VR, 3D printing, IoT, robotics, blockchain, and drones were coined by PwC as the "Essential Eight," in their earlier report. Eight years later, the firm updated its "Essential Eight," leaving out 3D printing and drones and adding quantum computing and neuromorphic computing (PwC, 2024).

These eight technologies that the firm identified are powerhouses on their own, but exponentially more impactful when merged together:

1. *Artificial Intelligence (AI):* Automates complex decision-making tasks to mimic human cognitive functions, from natural language processing used in customer service bots to predictive analytics in healthcare.

2. *Augmented Reality (AR):* Enhances the real world with digital overlays, helping technicians perform complex machinery repairs with real-time data and instructions projected directly onto their field of vision.

3. *Virtual Reality (VR):* Creates completely immersive environments for applications ranging from virtual property tours in real estate to advanced training simulations in aviation.

4. *Internet of Things (IoT):* Connects everyday objects to the Internet, enabling them to send and receive data, which optimizes everything from inventory management in retail to smart home automation.

5. *Robotics:* Employs machines to automate tasks, seen in applications such as robotic arms in manufacturing lines and autonomous robots in logistics and delivery.

6. *Blockchain:* Offers a secure, decentralized ledger for transactions, enhancing transparency and trust in processes like supply chain tracking and smart contracts in real estate transactions.

7. *Quantum Computing:* Enhances computers and applications like AI, optimization, and simulation, allowing them to perform complex operations and solve challenging problems much faster than traditional methods.

8. *Neuromorphic Computing:* Imitates the human brain's structure and function. It uses electronic circuits to replicate the brain's network of neurons and their interactions, moving beyond the simple binary on–off operations of traditional computing.

The Eight "Lions" Unite in the Quantum Era
Personalized Medicine

The Quantum Era is poised to fundamentally transform how we understand and treat the human body. Technology convergence, from AI to neuromorphic computing, promises not merely incremental advancements but a complete reimagination of medicine, healthcare, and the human condition. This synergy is shaping a future where medicine is not only personalized but is also more predictive, preventive, and precise.

AI is already pivotal in genomics, parsing vast datasets of genetic information with a speed and accuracy far beyond human capabilities. As AI grows more sophisticated, its predictive power sharpens, allowing for earlier detection and more precisely targeted treatments. Neuromorphic computing, which emulates the human brain's neural architecture, enhances these capabilities further, processing data with unprecedented efficiency and speed.

Blockchain technology introduces a new paradigm for data security and collaboration. It ensures that sensitive genetic information can be shared across global research networks without compromising patient privacy, facilitating a level of collaboration that was previously unattainable.

Quantum computing brings the promise of making the currently impossible possible, handling complex, multivariable problems that unlock new understandings of how genes interact with each other and with environmental factors. Such insights are expected to revolutionize personalized medicine, enabling the development of highly accurate disease prediction models and customized treatment plans.

AR and VR technologies are set to overhaul the educational experiences of both medical professionals and patients. These tools offer immersive simulations that help practitioners understand complex genetic conditions or enable patients to visualize how their genetic profiles might influence their health, leading to better-informed decisions about their treatment options.

This technological convergence will be able to address some of the most daunting health-related challenges:

- *Complex Genetic Disorders:* Technologies like AI and quantum computing will drive the development of treatments for conditions such as cystic fibrosis and muscular dystrophy, by enabling the analysis of how multiple genes interact to influence these diseases.

- *Multifactorial Diseases:* Diseases influenced by a combination of genetic, environmental, and lifestyle factors, such as diabetes and heart disease, will be being tackled more effectively through integrated approaches that use AI to analyze diverse datasets, allowing for preemptive health interventions.

- *Cancer Treatment:* AI will completely transform cancer treatment by tailoring protocols to the genetic makeup of individual patients, improving the efficacy of treatments. Simultaneously, blockchain technology ensures that the vast amounts of data generated remain secure and private, yet accessible where necessary.

- *Real-Time Health Monitoring and Intervention:* IoT and AR/VR will revolutionize how we monitor health and administer treatments. Imagine smart wearables not just tracking health metrics but predicting and automatically responding to potential health emergencies.

- *Mental Health:* Neuromorphic computing's advanced pattern recognition capabilities will enhance diagnostic accuracy in mental health, allowing for earlier and more tailored interventions.

The era ahead, empowered by these technological synergies, will make much of today's medicine appear as primitive as medieval practices seem to us now. Questions we ask ourselves now like "how did they not understand what germs were?" will soon be "how did they not understand how to prevent Alzheimer's?"

This new phase of "precision medicine" will offer treatments so specific and interventions so timely that they'll fundamentally change our approach to healthcare—from reactive to proactive. It is a redefinition of healthcare itself, promising a future where the full potential of medical science can be realized in ways we are only beginning to imagine.

Precise Climate Modeling

With climate change being the ultimate enemy, technology convergence will be the Voltron-like force we will need to offer humankind hope and actionable strategies to tackle this global crisis head-on. Technology convergence will change the way we approach, analyze, and intervene in Earth's delicate systems, collectively stretching the very fabric of what we thought was possible in climate modeling and environmental management.

We're already seeing AI algorithms predict complex climate patterns with a finesse that outstrips human capabilities, but adding blockchain to the mix will bring a new layer of trust and transparency to our environmental data. Quantum computing will be able to dive into vastly complicated environmental simulations that are not possible with classical computers, offering insights at a speed and scale that are truly transformative. Meanwhile, AR and VR will immerse us in future scenarios, making the abstract palpably immediate, and robotics combined with neuromorphic computing will reshape field research, allowing us to collect data in environments that are beyond human reach.

- *Hyperaccurate Weather Prediction and Disaster Response:* Leveraging quantum computing, we will be able to create advanced climate models that predict severe weather events months in advance with unprecedented accuracy. Integrating these models with AI, IoT sensors, and satellites allows for real-time severe weather predictions. AR/VR technologies will enable emergency planners to simulate impact scenarios and train response teams effectively, while robotics will be deployed to reinforce infrastructure predisaster and aid in search and rescue postdisaster, all coordinated through AI that dynamically adapts to evolving conditions.

- *Smart Grids for Renewable Energy:* AI and neuromorphic computing will transform the management of smart grids, making instantaneous decisions on energy distribution based on live demand and supply, crucial for integrating unpredictable renewable energy sources. This will all be underpinned by blockchain, which will ensure secure, transparent energy transactions, facilitating a decentralized market where consumers directly trade renewable energy. VR will enhance this setup by allowing real-time visualization of energy flows, improving management during critical periods.

- *Climate Adaptation in Agricultural Planning:* AI systems will utilize climate and local weather data to equip farmers with dynamic planting strategies that optimize yields and reduce environmental impacts. Quantum computing will then refine these strategies with real-time adjustments from satellite and ground sensor data. AR will directly aid farmers in the field with optimized planting techniques, while blockchain secures farming data, ensuring a transparent and sustainable agricultural supply chain.

- *Carbon Trading and Tracking Emissions:* Blockchain will create a transparent, immutable ledger for carbon credit trading and emissions tracking, integrated with AI to predict and optimize market transactions. Quantum computing will accelerate the analysis of investment strategies and emission reduction methods, enabling companies to make informed, timely decisions in the carbon market.

Together, these technologies don't just change the game—they set a new playing field where the stakes are the very future of our planet. The tools that will be at our disposal equip us to engage with climate challenges in more direct and effective ways, promising not just to manage the crisis but to master our responses to it. In this arena, knowledge isn't just power; it's a pathway to sustainability.

Securing the Future with Quantum and Blockchain

As cybersecurity threats evolve, the combination of quantum computing and blockchain could create formidable defenses. Quantum computing might one day crack current encryption models, but it could also develop new, unbreakable forms of encryption for blockchain systems, safeguarding everything from financial transactions to private communications.

When these technologies are woven together, they create a unified ecosystem characterized by secure, transparent data flows. This ecosystem is the bedrock upon which intelligent, ultraefficient applications and services can be built. The promise of this ecosystem lies in its ability to deliver solutions that are not only secure and personalized but also deeply rooted in trust. Through the collective strength of these technologies, we stand on the brink of a new era of digital transformation, one that is as boundless in its innovation as it is grounded in security and intelligence.

Convergence in the Real World

For now, the rudimentary version of what the convergence effect is generally called the Metaverse. Many aspects of this virtual world are already in use and in plain sight for all to witness. While Mark Zuckerberg may have overdramatized the Metaverse's potential with videos of virtual concerts via Meta, the convergence of the Quantum Revolution's key pillars (PwC's "Essential Eight") are already being integrated into our work and personal lives. In fact, today 77% of the world's population uses an AI-powered device or service, even though only 33% are aware of this (IBM, 2023).

Services like Microsoft Mesh offer virtual collaboration in a shared holographic space using AR and VR to allow colleagues to interact as if they are in the same room (Microsoft Research, 2023). Wearable devices like the Apple Watch and Fitbit track various health metrics, including heart rate, sleep patterns, and physical activity. These devices use AI to provide personalized health insights and recommendations. Telemedicine platforms such as Teladoc and Doctor on Demand allow patients to consult with healthcare professionals remotely with secure video conferencing that also integrates with electronic health records. Smart appliances like Samsung's Family Hub refrigerator and Whirlpool's smart ovens are connected to the Internet and can be controlled via apps offering features such as recipe suggestions based on the food available, remote monitoring, and energy management.

The journey of progress and convergence will transform into something that is much more comprehensive and immersive than our conception of the Metaverse now. It will be so pervasive that it won't even be called the Metaverse. It will be our life.

As we stand now, in the early stages of the Quantum Era's technology convergence, we can clearly see where all of this is headed. While disjointed and dumped now, the journey of what we call the Metaverse now will progress, converge, and transform into something that is much more comprehensive and immersive. It will be so pervasive that it won't even be called the Metaverse. It will be our life.

A Day in a Technologically Integrated World

Imagine a world where your morning coffee is prepared by a smart kitchen that predicts the exact time you wake up, the medicine you take is tailored to your DNA and synthesized in your bathroom, and your commute to work is coordinated by an autonomous vehicle that communicates with every other car on the road to ensure the quickest, safest route to your destination.

This isn't a scene from a sci-fi movie; it's a near-future reality made possible by the seamless integration of technologies like AI, blockchain, IoT, AR/VR, robotics, and quantum computing. In this envisioned future, each technology does not stand alone but is interwoven into a fabric of everyday life, enhancing efficiency and personalization at every turn.

As you wake, sensors adjust the lighting and temperature based on your preferences and the weather outside. Your AI assistant greets you with an overview of your schedule, optimized in real-time through learning algorithms that adapt to your preferences and priorities. As you get ready, your health monitoring devices provide a tailored health update and nutrition advice, seamlessly integrated into your electronic medical records, secure and up-to-date, thanks to blockchain technology.

On this particular morning, your child wakes up feeling under the weather. Instead of scrambling to assess the situation under stress, your home's health monitoring system has already noted slight changes in their temperature and sleeping patterns overnight. Before you even step out of bed, you receive a gentle notification from your AI health assistant. It suggests a light breakfast for your child, rich in nutrients to boost immunity, and has already adjusted your smart thermostat to a more comfortable temperature to ease your child's symptoms.

An appointment with a pediatrician is scheduled via a telemedicine platform integrated with your home's system. Your child doesn't even have to leave their bed. A quick AR-enabled consultation begins, with the doctor reviewing real-time data collected through wearable sensors. The doctor prescribes medication, which is automatically sent to your local pharmacy for drone delivery within the hour. All the while, your child is comforted in the familiar environment of home, with you by their side instead of navigating a hectic morning rush to a doctor's office.

Since the care of your under-the-weather child has been taken care of for now, you realize you're late to the office (if you still happen to go to one). As you step outside, your autonomous vehicle syncs with your calendar and current traffic data to suggest the best route. Roads are smart, with IoT devices embedded throughout the infrastructure, communicating real-time conditions to all nearby vehicles, vastly reducing the risk of accidents and traffic jams. Meanwhile, smart roads charge your autonomous EV as you drive.

You made it to work. Sensors recognize your car and signal your arrival, automatically opening the gate. Your vehicle communicates with the building's parking system to find an optimal parking spot. As you walk to the office, personalized settings adjust the lighting and temperature along your path to your preferences, which are securely stored and continuously optimized via blockchain technology.

At your workstation, an IoT-enabled environment has already adjusted everything to your liking, thanks to predictive AI that learns your preferences. Your chair, desk height, and even monitor settings adjust automatically. As you settle in, a virtual dashboard appears, projected by AR technology, displaying your day's schedule, key notifications, and project statuses in an interactive, visually enriched format.

For your first meeting, you put on VR goggles that transport you to a virtual meeting room. Here, colleagues from across the globe appear as if they were sitting right next to you, complete with real-time language translation and data visualization. This technology not only saves travel time and costs but also enhances collaborative efforts with tools that allow for the manipulation of digital objects and data within this shared virtual space.

Even your breaks are enhanced. For lunch, you head to the cafeteria where IoT devices have already prepped your meal based on your dietary preferences logged in the company's wellness program. During lunch, an optional short VR meditation session helps you destress, personalized to your mental state monitored through wearable devices.

Later, you might join a training session. Here, VR capabilities simulate real-world scenarios that are too costly or impractical to recreate physically, such as high-risk emergency procedures or intricate technical equipment operations. This not only enhances learning outcomes but also provides a safe, cost-effective environment for continuous professional development.

117

Throughout the day, AI assistants suggest optimization strategies for your projects, pulling in the latest market research and analytics. They schedule follow-ups and manage your time efficiently, all the while ensuring your data is encrypted and secured by blockchain, maintaining confidentiality across all communications and transactions.

As your workday concludes, systems automatically wrap up tasks, secure all data, and prepare summaries for the next day. Your AI assistant notifies you of the best time to leave based on traffic patterns and weather conditions, syncing perfectly with your smart vehicle for a smooth commute home.

Meanwhile, back at home, your other child is struggling with a complex science project. They activate a holographic tutor, summoned via voice command to an AI assistant. This tutor not only explains the scientific concepts interactively but also uses AR to project experiments right onto the kitchen table, making abstract ideas tangible and engaging.

Concurrently, your spouse decides to try a new recipe for dinner. Mid-preparation, they discover a missing ingredient. A quick voice command to the home AI sends an order to a local grocery service. The ingredient, along with suggested alternatives based on past purchases and dietary preferences, is delivered by a drone within minutes, ensuring the cooking process remains uninterrupted.

Blockchain technology underpins these interactions by securing medical records and financial transactions throughout the day, ensuring they are seamless, secure, and unnoticed. It supports the privacy and compliance needed for medical consultations and streamlines payments and refunds for the automated delivery services, creating a frictionless and reliable infrastructure.

As the day comes to a close, your home's environment continues to adapt to ensure a comfortable and healing space for your recovering child, monitored and managed by integrated health monitoring systems, while you and your partner get personalized recommendations for a new streaming series you haven't seen. Your smart devices then remind you of your ideal bedtime and set your alarm for the next morning.

Summary

This interconnected future holds the promise of making our lives more connected and our economies more robust, all while respecting individual privacy and enhancing security. It's a world where technology acts almost as a sixth sense, enhancing human capabilities and allowing us to achieve greater efficiency and harmony in our lives.

If this all sounds a bit Utopian, it is. As exciting as this future is, it requires a collective, global response to tackle some incredibly daunting challenges. Careful consideration—ethical, regulatory, and social—is required by our generation, the creators and arbiters of this technology, to ensure that these tools are integrated in ways that improve well-being, foster equity, and move future generations forward. The responsibility lies not just with technologists and policymakers but with all of us to guide this technology in ways that enhance rather than encroach, that democratize rather than divide. The lessons from Voltron are clear: unite in purpose, integrate with intention, and always wield the resulting power with a deep sense of responsibility.

The convergence of these technologies isn't just about making our lives easier or more efficient. It's about reimagining the potential of human-machine collaboration that goes well beyond catchy names and utopian fantasy lands. Our future in the Quantum Era won't need a name because it will simply be life as we know it. Just as our children today look perplexed at a rotary phone or a DVD, their children (and children's children) will live in a world where today's novel and exciting technologies will mature to become the mundane and unnoticed of tomorrow. Wealth is created by those that can capitalize on the convergence and maturation of revolutionary innovations before they get too boring.

CHAPTER 6

Technology Life Cycles, Waves, and Darwinism

The technology life cycle is as critical to grasping the nuances of innovation as understanding compound interest is to mastering personal finance. Think of it as the lifespan of a technology, from the moment it's a twinkle in an inventor's eye to its last gasp before being edged out by something sleeker, faster, better. This journey is loaded with potential and pitfalls—a thrilling ride through initial promise drowning in uncertainty, a surge of growth as the market catches on, reaching the zenith of maturity, and then eventually an inevitable decline as the next big thing arrives.

It's a cycle of economic Darwinism: innovate or die. Technologies that adapt and evolve can survive longer, but no technology remains at the top forever. Newcomers, armed with fresher insights and less baggage, eventually dethrone the old guard, pushing them into the annals of history. This isn't just about gadgets getting obsolete; it's about understanding market dynamics, consumer behavior, and investment strategy. Every phase of the technology life cycle offers unique opportunities and challenges, and the winners are those who leverage this knowledge to their advantage, be it through investing in potential breakthroughs or knowing when to pull back.

© Tal Elyashiv 2025
T. Elyashiv, *Investing in Revolutions*, https://doi.org/10.1007/979-8-8688-1177-7_6

As President John F. Kennedy once said, "Change is the law of life and those who look only to the past or present are certain to miss the future" (Kennedy, 1963).

When Technologies Grow Up

Even with today's compressed adoption cycles, the process to achieve maturity and ubiquity takes wins and losses, death and rebirth, along with a host of visionaries. In fact, the life cycle of any given technology closely resembles that of a human's (see Figure 6-1).

In its infancy, a technology is just emerging, its potential unclear and its structure underdeveloped, much like a newborn. During this phase, its survival is uncertain, and it requires significant nurturing to stabilize. As it enters the growth phase, the technology, akin to a child growing into adolescence and then adulthood, begins to show its true potential. It becomes more robust, its place in the market starts to solidify, and it is increasingly adopted.

Maturity arrives when the technology has been fully integrated into the market; it's widely used and its features are well understood, much like a person reaching their peak in middle age.

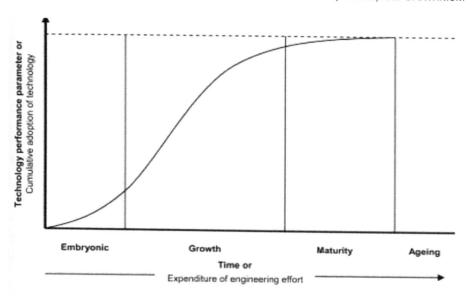

Figure 6-1. *Technology Life Cycle: A visual representation comparing human life stages to technology development phases, showing the parallel progression through infancy, growth, maturity, and decline. Source: "Technology Lifecycle Management" (Gartner Research, 2023)*

A key sign that a technology has reached maturity is a slowdown in the pace of groundbreaking advancements. With immature technologies, developments tend to be rapid and transformative, frequently altering the technology's foundational architecture or its application paradigms. In contrast, enhancements to a mature technology are typically incremental, focusing on refining and improving existing capabilities rather than redefining them.

Consider the QWERTY keyboard design. Developed in the nineteenth century and refined over the years, the QWERTY layout has remained largely unchanged for over a century. Its typing speeds and error rates have been extensively studied and optimized, making it a staple of modern typing interfaces. Despite various attempts to introduce more efficient layouts, QWERTY has persisted, proving that stability and familiarity can often outweigh marginal gains in efficiency.

Additional indicators of technological maturity include widespread adoption by industries and consumers, high levels of usability for experts and novices alike, seamless integration with other established technologies, and stable costs for associated devices and infrastructure. Another telling sign is a decrease in overall hype around the technology, suggesting that it has become a normalized part of everyday life rather than a novel curiosity.

The life cycle pattern underscores that the initial hype is necessary for market penetration. It sparks innovation and draws in investment, demonstrating potential applications that extend beyond the novelty. However, it is after the initial excitement has subsided that the technology evolves and matures, integrating deeply into various sectors and beginning to yield significant financial returns. This phase often serves as a barometer, testing the adaptability and relevance of the technology within broader socio-economic contexts.

It's also important to note that like humans, while there are four distinct technology life stages, no two are exactly alike. Typically, the technology life cycle chart looks like an S-curves (see Figure 6-1), expecting a smooth and predictable path from obscurity to ubiquity. Yet, the real world is messier thanks to the myriad of critical force field factors. Some technologies sprint from infancy to adolescence, while others linger in their formative years, slow to "cross the chasm" and find their market fit.

Take quantum computing, for example. Due to a variety of factors including high costs and scalability, quantum computing has been unable to move past the infancy stage (as of where we stand in 2024). However, a technology like the internal combustion engine has remained in the maturity stage (with obvious incremental improvements over time) for more than a century.

To create a more holistic view, it's helpful to refer back to Rogers' Adoption Curve as much of the time spent in each life stage has much to do with the progression of adoption—from Innovators and Early Adopters to Late Majority and Laggards. For instance, a technology in the growth phase of its life cycle might currently be appealing to the Early Majority segment of the adoption curve, while appealing to the Late Majority may signal a lengthy stage in maturity.

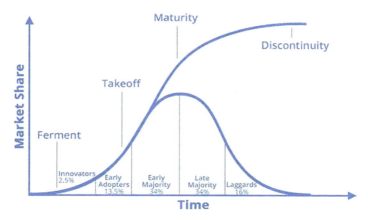

Figure 2: The tech adoption life cycle on top of a graph of total users (S-Curve). Source.

Figure 6-2. *Technology Adoption and Life Cycle Integration: Illustration showing the relationship between Rogers' Adoption Curve and technology life cycle stages. Source: "Diffusion of Innovations" (Rogers, 2003)*

But does this maturity equate to obsolescence or a lack of excitement? Not necessarily. In fact, mature technologies often provide the backbone for further innovation and convergence, proving that being "boring" is not synonymous with being irrelevant or unworthy of investment.

The Stealth Power of Mature Technologies: Apple Makes Boring Sexy

In the rapid pace of today's tech life cycles, there's a profound power in the mundane. These aren't the show ponies of the tech world but the workhorses—reliable, efficient, and incredibly integral to our routines.

And nobody plays this game better than Apple, a company that's turned the art of making technology indispensable (a.k.a. boring) into a blockbuster business model.

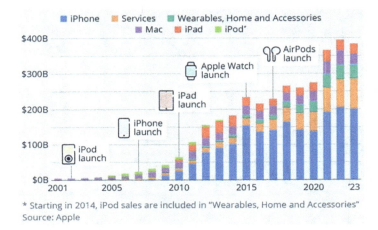

* Starting in 2014, iPod sales are included in "Wearables, Home and Accessories"
Source: Apple

Figure 6-3. *Apple's Technology Maturation Strategy: Visual representation of Apple's approach to technology refinement and market maturation. Source: "Apple's Innovation Strategy" (Harvard Business Review, 2023)*

Imagine life without the intuitive taps on your iPhone or the seamless integration of your MacBook into both work and play. Apple doesn't just sell gadgets; they sell your next indispensable life partner in tech form. It's the kind of evolution in technology that Bill Gates predicted when he said, "the advance of technology is based on making it fit in so that you don't really even notice it, so it's part of everyday life." Apple epitomizes this, embedding technology so deeply into the fabric of our daily routines that its absence feels like a missing limb.

But getting technology to this point of "boring brilliance" is no small feat. It requires a mastery of the market, an understanding of consumer behavior, and the foresight to see beyond current trends. Apple nails this, time and again, by refining and perfecting the user experience with each new product iteration—making previous versions feel suddenly clunky and outdated, not by reinventing the wheel but by polishing it to a standard that's hard to live without.

The path to making technology essential and invisible is riddled with challenges—from navigating regulatory mazes to pacing the bleeding edge of innovation without bleeding out. Apple masters this. They don't just push tech forward; they make it indispensable, embedding it so deeply into our routines that it feels like a basic utility, and ultimately turning "boring" into billions.

Apple didn't invent headphones, but they did innovate and transform this existing technology into AirPods which soared to sustained maturity quickly becoming an almost unnoticeable extension of the human body at this stage. In fact, if Apple AirPods was a stand-alone company, it would have a market capitalization of nearly $300 billion, making it the 26th largest company in the world (Morgan Stanley Research, 2024).

Figure 6-4. *AirPods Market Value Comparison: Chart comparing AirPods' market value to major global companies. Source: Bernstein Research (2024)*

Apple is at it again with Apple Intelligence. While there are no crystal balls to proclaim its AI strategy a success, what is evident is that based on its track record, the company can turn today's AI infancy into mature AI for the masses.

Apple's strategy of being "the second mouse that gets the cheese" is clear, according to professor and author Scott Galloway: "Take something invented elsewhere; make it more consumer friendly, easier to use, and more reliable; mix in world-class industrial design; and print billions" (Galloway, S., 2024).

All in all, Apple doesn't just use technology to create products; they use it to create dependencies. The company's success also isn't just about making the present delightful but in forestalling their own obsolescence (Apple Inc., 2024). This, in a nutshell, is the power of mature technology: not merely to exist but to become essential.

Technology Darwinism: Decline, Waves, and Creative Destruction

Much like the various stages in human life, the technology life cycle has distinct phases, albeit with considerable variability and unexpected turns. As previously mentioned, the path to maturity is nonlinear. And while reaching tech maturity and the ultimate prize of being deemed "boring," something happens. It's similar to reaching our human "twilight years." For some, this phase might come on rapidly; for others, it's a slow fade. But make no mistake, just as every person faces their inevitable decline, so too does every technology.

Decline happens when a new technology begins to overshadow the old. As emerging technologies offer better alternatives, demand for the matured technology wanes. This is not necessarily because the old technology gets worse; its performance might still improve, but the relative advantages of new technologies in a changing world are greater.

The Decline: An Inevitable Phase

Every technology, no matter how groundbreaking, is on a timer. The decline phase in the technology life cycle isn't just an ending—it's a transformation. It's where mature technologies, having peaked in both utility and market saturation, face the new kids on the block: technologies that are faster, more efficient, or simply more in tune with the shifting demands of society.

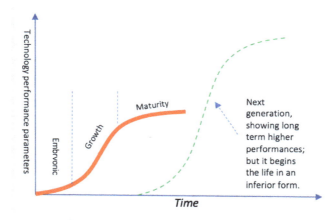

Figure 6-5. *Technology Decline Pattern: Visualization showing how emerging technologies overtake mature ones during the decline phase. Source: "The Technology Lifecycle and Market Evolution" (MIT Technology Review, 2024)*

This phase marks a critical juncture where established technologies start to cede ground to emerging ones. As one technology reaches its zenith and begins to coast toward obsolescence, somewhere in the wings, a core technology is brewing, ready to disrupt the status quo.

Once a towering force in the tech landscape, PCs have seen their central role in our digital lives gradually fade. But the decline of the PC isn't because of a lack of innovation, it's because of the rise of mobile devices like smartphones and tablets. The PC isn't extinct, but its dominance has waned, reshaped by a world that values connectivity and mobility over stationary hardware.

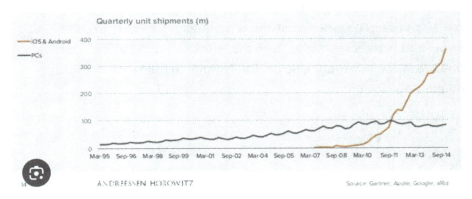

Figure 6-6. *PC Market Evolution: Historical trend of PC market share versus mobile devices. Source: IDC Global Device Tracker (2024)*

Smelling Smoke Before the Fire: Navigating the Decline

Navigating a technology's decline is as crucial as harnessing its ascent. Companies at the forefront of technological waves must not only innovate but also possess an acute foresight to foresee their own obsolescence. Understanding when a technology is beginning to ebb is pivotal, as the decline phase, while inevitable, offers opportunities for those prepared to adapt.

The key challenge here is anticipation. Companies, and investors in them, need to recognize the subtle signals of change: the emergence of new competitors, shifts in consumer behavior, or advancements in underlying technologies. Recognizing these signs requires a deep understanding of force field factors—economic, cultural, regulatory, and technological dynamics that can accelerate or hinder a technology's relevance.

For instance, regulatory changes can abruptly alter the landscape, making some technologies obsolete while catapulting others to the forefront. Economic shifts can suddenly shift funding and consumer spending, reshaping the market's demands. Technological breakthroughs can render old solutions cumbersome or unnecessary, and cultural shifts can lead to a change in consumer preferences and expectations.

The NVIDIA Story: Masterclass in Disruptive Innovation and the Ultimate Decline Pivot

In the late 1990s and early 2000s, NVIDIA was a notable player in the graphics card industry, primarily enhancing the visual experience of video games. They were good, really good, at what they did, but as the tech landscape evolved, so too did the risks of becoming just another chipmaker lost in the sea of commoditization.

Just as NVIDIA could have settled into a comfortable decline, resting on the laurels of being a top-tier provider for gamers, they pivoted. They saw an emerging wave not yet on the mainstream radar—deep learning and AI—and they jumped on it. But this wasn't just a slight shift in direction; it was a strategic overhaul that required betting big on a future that was anything but certain.

As AI and deep learning began to explode, fueled by an insatiable demand for processing power, NVIDIA's GPUs became the de facto engine driving it all. NVIDIA's chips became essential for AI research labs, tech giants, and startups pushing into machine learning, cementing their role as not just participants but leaders in the AI revolution (Bloomberg Financial Data, 2024).

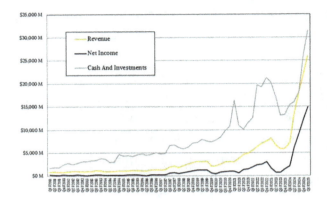

Figure 6-7. *NVIDIA's Market Performance: NVIDIA's stock performance and market value growth through strategic pivot to AI. Source: Bloomberg Financial Markets (2024)*

Today, NVIDIA stands as a behemoth in the tech industry, a key player in everything from gaming and automobiles to healthcare and data centers. Their near-miss with decline is not just a tale of recovery but a playbook on how to leverage foresight, adaptability, and strategic courage to not just survive but thrive.

Thus, the art of navigating decline is not just about spotting the decline but actively preparing for it. Moreover, understanding force field factors isn't just about defense—it's about playing a smarter offense. Companies that can adeptly navigate these complex dynamics can not only withstand the decline of one technology but can also lead the charge in the next technological revolution. It's about being at the right place, at the right time, with the right toolset.

Technology Waves: The Tides of Change

The life cycle of a technology is inherently linked to technology waves—those sweeping advances that redefine industries. These waves come with their own momentum, powered by innovation and the cumulative buildup of enhancements that make the old ways increasingly untenable. For instance, the cloud computing wave has revolutionized how we store and manage data, pushing aside traditional on-premise servers and solutions.

These waves don't just introduce new technologies; they fundamentally alter the consumer expectations and industry standards. As each wave crests, it washes away the entrenched technologies that can no longer keep pace, no matter how deeply they are embedded in the consumer consciousness.

It's true that these waves are about the exciting possibilities of new ideas and innovations—a renewal of sorts. But they are also destructive— decimating industries, jobs and capital in their wake. Yet, while some jobs vanish, others emerge as part of the evolution of adoption. For investors, those riding the wave can see significant returns, but hanging onto the past can mean watching your investments evaporate.

In his aforementioned newsletter, Scott Galloway crunches some specific data on disruptive innovation. As he puts it, "the kind that marks a "before" and "after" in our lives — is terrible for shareholder value." He also lists some innovators that, if old enough, some of us could recognize but did not have the staying power to overcome their eventual demise. This includes companies like Seattle Computer Products, Xerox PARC, Grid, Palm, Netscape, Friendster, Blackberry, Alta Vista, and Nokia, with a combined market capitalization of $21 billion. As Galloway notes, the companies that capitalized on the next technological wave that the incumbents helped drive, including Microsoft, Apple, Google, and Meta, register a market capitalization of $7+ trillion.

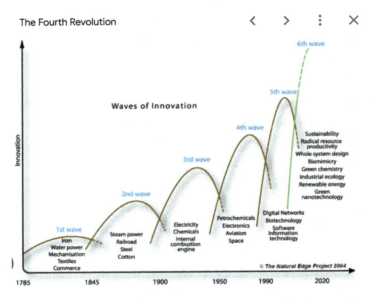

Figure 6-8. *Technology Wave Progression: Historical progression of technology waves from Industrial to Quantum Revolution. Source: World Economic Forum "Future of Technology" Report (2024)*

Technology waves are not just about new gadgets; they signify profound societal, economic, and cultural shifts. Each wave reshapes our world, from the Industrial Revolution, which transitioned us from hand production to mechanization and spurred urbanization and modern capitalism, to the Digital Revolution that globalized information and transformed communication.

Now, we are at the dawn of the Quantum Revolution, marked by advances in artificial intelligence, blockchain, and Internet of Things (IoT), among others. This wave is not just enhancing individual sectors but is defining a new way of life, integrating technology into everything, from healthcare to global connectivity.

Creative Destruction: The Fire That Renews

As evident in Figure 6-9, they are a forward-moving pattern that requires one wave to subside while another builds in dominance.

Joseph Schumpeter's concept of creative destruction provides the framework for understanding this phase of decline and renewal (Schumpeter, J. A., 1942). It's the economic forest fire—the inferno force that clears out the old to make way for the new. This isn't destruction for its own sake; it's an essential part of the economic cycle, vital for purging inefficiency and sparking innovation (McKinsey Global Institute, 2024). Each wave of technological innovation can be seen as a force of creative destruction, tearing down barriers and old practices to create space for new growth and opportunities.

The speed at which creative destruction unfolds can vary wildly. It's dictated not just by the innovation itself but by a complex relationship of market forces, consumer behaviors, and regulatory frameworks. Some industries get flipped overnight, while others change with the sluggishness of continental drift.

A quintessential example of creative destruction happening swiftly is the rise of streaming music services, particularly the seismic impact of Spotify on the music retail industry. This transformation wasn't gradual; it was meteoric and fundamentally altered the landscape within a few short years.

Before Spotify's launch in 2008, music consumers primarily bought physical albums or downloaded tracks from platforms like iTunes. However, Spotify's introduction of streaming music as a subscription service changed everything rapidly. By offering unlimited access to a vast library of music for a monthly fee, Spotify rendered buying individual albums or tracks nearly obsolete for a significant portion of the market (Spotify Technology S.A., 2023).

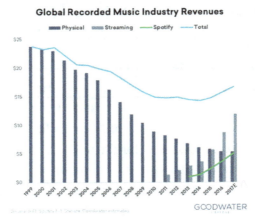

Figure 6-9. *Music Industry Transformation: Revenue shift from physical media to streaming services. Source: RIAA Annual Revenue Report (2024)*

The speed of this shift was staggering. By providing instant access to music without the need for physical storage or individual purchases, Spotify not only catered to consumer desires for convenience and variety but also capitalized on the ubiquity of smartphones and improved Internet connectivity. Major record stores and traditional music distribution channels felt the impact almost immediately, with many experiencing sharp declines in physical and download sales.

In contrast, the promise of the electric vehicle's road to dominance has been clogged with obstacles—lack of charging infrastructure, high initial costs, consumer range anxiety, and slowly shifting regulatory landscapes. Tesla might be charging ahead, but the complete overhaul of the auto industry is a marathon, not a sprint. It's an evolution happening at a pace that allows for adjustment and adaptation, not just for companies but for consumers and regulators too.

The variance in these timelines boils down to force field factors. Regulatory support, technological readiness, consumer acceptance, and market infrastructure either accelerate or brake the speed of creative destruction. Spotify stormed the market because it aligned perfectly with an ecosystem ripe for change. EVs meanwhile are navigating a minefield of logistical and societal hurdles, making their journey to market supremacy a more measured advance.

Disruptive Innovation: The Fuel That Flames the Fire

The technology life cycle offers a road map of a technology's progression, with technology waves providing the context of this progression within broader trends, and the theory of creative destruction highlights the inevitable obsolescence and replacement cycles within these waves. And then, there's the concept of disruptive innovation, which explains the mechanics of market upheaval and industry transformation.

American academic and business consultant Clayton Christensen's theory of disruptive innovation specifically looks at how simpler, more affordable products can eventually displace established technologies (Christensen, C. M., 2015). Initially, these innovations are often overlooked by incumbent leaders, which mistakenly perceive them as inferior or targeting only the most marginal customer segments. However, before they even know it, these disruptive innovations evolve, grow in adoption, and eventually spell the demise of the incumbent—sometimes before the old guard is able to pivot or adapt.

Disruptive innovations are typically the brainchildren of outsiders and startups, not the behemoths leading the market. Why? Because the established corporate leadership is a bit too cozy raking in profits from existing products to gamble on unproven ideas. These giants are prisoners of their own success, handcuffed to incremental improvements that defend their turf rather than explorations that could expand it. Disruptive innovations, with their dismal initial returns and resource-sucking development, are left to agile, hungry startups that can operate below the radar.

The disruptive technologies that often spell trouble for established companies aren't typically groundbreaking or technologically novel. In fact, they are usually iterations or improvements on the incumbents. However, they share two crucial characteristics: firstly, they usually offer a different set of performance attributes that initially don't appeal to existing customers. Secondly, these attributes evolve rapidly, allowing the technology to quickly meet and then exceed the needs of those initial markets.

Disruptive Innovators zero in on how smaller companies with fewer resources manage to successfully challenge established incumbents. Disruptive innovation is sneaky; it often starts in niches or overlooked markets. The innovation doesn't appear threatening at first, which is why it's underestimated by bigger players. But as it evolves, it reshapes the industry landscape, often drastically reducing costs or creating a new market altogether (Journal of Innovation Management, 2024). Disruptive innovations don't burn down forests; they grow quietly in the underbrush until they're strong enough to take over the ecosystem.

Creative Destruction vs. Disruptive Innovation: Siblings in the Technology Revolution Family

While both processes involve significant change and the displacement of established systems, the key difference between creative destruction and disruptive innovation is their origin and impact. Creative destruction is broader and more inevitable; it's a macroeconomic principle that affects industries as a whole and is driven by internal and external forces beyond sheer innovation—like economic shifts, societal changes, and technological advancements. It's the old making way for the new in a cycle of renewal that keeps markets vibrant and competitive.

Disruptive innovation, on the other hand, is more micro, focused on specific sectors or companies. It's about strategic innovation creating new markets or reshaping existing ones, often before anyone else notices there's a game to be played. This type of innovation isn't just about technology; it's about business models and market strategies. It's about delivering accessible products or services that open up a previously untapped customer base, or dramatically lower costs, making products affordable and accessible to a wider audience.

While Spotify has proven to be a formidable Creative Destructor, Netflix is a prime example of a Disruptive Innovator—a case study in the stealth rise, and inevitable dominance, of a revolutionary technology that changed business models and consumer behavior. Here's the story of how a DVD rental service transformed into a streaming juggernaut, effectively putting the final nails in the coffin of Blockbuster and similar enterprises.

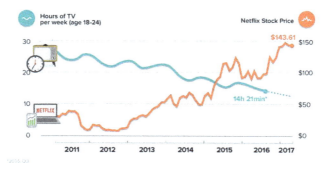

Figure 6-10. *Netflix Subscriber Growth: Netflix's growth trajectory from DVD rental to streaming dominance. Source: Netflix Shareholder Letters (2000–2024)*

In the late 1990s, Netflix began its journey, modestly distributing DVDs by mail in those now-iconic red envelopes. This was a time when Blockbuster dominated the scene with its brick-and-mortar rental stores, raking in profits from rental fees and notorious late charges. But Netflix was setting the stage for a major upheaval. They recognized the potential of the Internet—still in its early days for streaming video—and they seized the opportunity, transitioning from a mail-order service to a pioneering streaming platform. This shift wasn't just an improvement; it was a complete reinvention of how media could be consumed. But it was an incremental change.

Netflix's early bet on streaming was bold and forward-thinking. The company's approach exemplifies disruptive innovation at its core. They dismantled the traditional video rental model, eliminating the need for physical stores and late fees, offering instead the convenience of unlimited, on-demand viewing. This was a game-changer, offering a new level of accessibility and convenience that rendered the old ways obsolete (Netflix Financial Reports, 2000–2024).

The ripple effects of Netflix's strategy were profound. Blockbuster found itself outpaced and eventually obsolete. Cable companies scrambled to offer competitive on-demand services, and the film and TV industries adapted, developing content for the binge-watching culture that Netflix popularized.

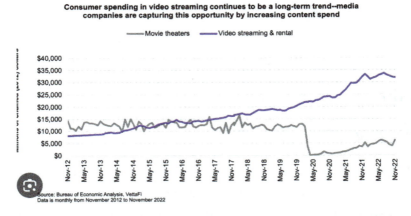

Figure 6-11. *Streaming Market Evolution Description: Market share distribution among streaming services. Source: Digital Entertainment Group (2024)*

The Technology Life Cycle: Driving Economic Prosperity

The technology life cycle is not just an academic concept but a practical tool for understanding how innovations rise and fall. It frames the continual process of technological renewal that drives modern economies, reminding us that today's cutting-edge innovations will, even with long-lasting phases of maturity and widespread adoption, inevitably become tomorrow's case studies in obsolescence.

As we look toward the future, particularly with transformative pillars like AI and blockchain in the Quantum Revolution, it becomes increasingly important to not only understand these technologies but also to anticipate how they will evolve and intersect. This period will see massive innovative shifts over the next few decades but not in the ways you think and not on the timeline that's assumed. Flying cars and robot nannies are fun but outlandish. Most of the transformational change will occur in unassuming sectors like manufacturing, transportation, energy grids, and pharmaceuticals. These sectors operate not to inspire but to optimize economic efficiency. It is within these nondescript settings that the most profound and life-altering innovations will create the next wave of change and opportunity for wealth creation.

Yet, while technology itself is a powerful agent of change, it is the companies behind these technologies that orchestrate their rise and fall. Just as it was from the Industrial Revolution through the Digital Revolution, it will be the companies and their leaders, from startup entrepreneurs to seasoned executives, that will define and drive the future of our global economy. The organizations that embrace the complexity of the technology life cycle, technology waves, and the onslaught of Creative Destructors and Disruptive Innovators won't just move markets; they'll create them.

Summary

The technology life cycle isn't just a theoretical framework—it's a living blueprint of how innovation shapes our world. What makes this particularly relevant today is how the Quantum Revolution is accelerating these cycles, compressing timelines while expanding possibilities.

The case studies of Apple, NVIDIA, and Netflix aren't just corporate success stories; they're masterclasses in navigating technological evolution. They teach us that survival isn't about being first—it's about being adaptable. In the face of creative destruction and disruptive innovation, the winners aren't always the pioneers but those who can read the signs of change and position themselves accordingly.

The future belongs not to those who can predict it, but to those who can adapt to its rhythms, recognize its patterns, and harness the power of both mature and emerging technologies to create value. In this era of rapid change, the most valuable skill isn't just innovation—it's the ability to navigate the complex balance between stability and disruption, between the proven and the possible.

CHAPTER 7

Technology Revolutions' Cast of Corporate Characters

Industry does not respect tradition–it only respects innovation.

—Satya Nadella (Microsoft CEO keynote speech, 2015)

The technology life cycle is not just a narrative about gadgets and software evolving in isolation—it is about the companies that cultivate, compete within, and sometimes crumble under the weight of these innovations. This cycle charts a course from the spark of inception through maturity and decline, as well as the waves of creative renewal and destruction. It's a cycle that sometimes rhymes but never repeats in the same way, with each turn driven not merely by the technologies themselves but by the vibrant ecosystem of businesses that develop, deploy, and sometimes destroy them.

This dynamic ecosystem is populated by distinct categories of corporate actors, each playing specialized roles in the drama of innovation. **Originators** are the pioneers, the bold first movers who envision and engineer the initial breakthroughs that disrupt the status quo. **Creative Destructors** then take the stage, challenging and demolishing established frameworks to clear the path for new growth. Parallel to this, **Disruptive**

T. Elyashiv, *Investing in Revolutions*, https://doi.org/10.1007/979-8-8688-1177-7_7

Innovators weave together existing threads of technology to spin new solutions, often starting from the fringes and moving to redefine entire industries. **Beneficiaries** adeptly capitalize on the shifting landscape, integrating new technologies into the fabric of everyday life and reaping the economic rewards as those technologies grow and mature. Meanwhile, the **Casualties**—those unable or unwilling to adapt—serve as cautionary tales of innovation's unforgiving pace.

Understanding these roles offers a clearer view of the technological zeitgeist, highlighting not just the creation of technology but the competitive and sometimes destructive environment in which this creation occurs.

Originators: The Vanguard of Innovation

If I had asked people what they wanted, they would have said faster horses.

—Henry Ford (Ford Motors Archives, 1922)

Originators plant the seeds of innovation, introducing groundbreaking technologies that open new possibilities and assumptions and viewpoints by employing a blend of foresight, understanding of environmental factors, and strategic scaling to cultivate widespread adoption and success.

Originators are the pioneers of each of the eras of technology revolutions (i.e., Mechanical, Electrical, and Digital Age), the first movers who introduce the core technologies that open up new frontiers. These are the creators—people like Tim Berners-Lee inventing the World Wide Web or the teams behind the early development of the silicon chip. These technologies themselves may not immediately transform society, but without these foundational breakthroughs, the initial tech earthquakes, the later aftershocks, and waves of innovation wouldn't be possible.

Operating often on the fringes of technology and market viability, Originators push the boundaries of what is known and possible. They venture into uncharted territories, not just solving existing problems but uncovering new potentials and opportunities. This daring to chart the unknown is fraught with risks but also opens the door to monumental shifts in technological capabilities and applications.

These pioneers are typically found in environments conducive to radical thinking and experimentation—be it in academic labs, startups brimming with disruptive ideas, or within innovative teams in established companies. They develop the first viable prototypes and concepts, proving the potential of technologies that can fundamentally alter landscapes.

For instance, IBM's development of the personal computer laid down the very fabric of today's computing world. As Originators, they not only introduced a new product but established a platform that would become central to the development of software and hardware innovations by countless others (IBM Annual Report, 2024).

Originators set the initial benchmarks and parameters for new technologies. They address fundamental challenges, provide proofs of concept, and demonstrate the viability of ideas that pave the way for expansive future innovations. Without these pioneers, the trajectory of technological advancement would lack a foundational starting point, crucial for the cascading progress we witness across industries today.

While we cannot be certain at this early stage in the Quantum Revolution who the Creative Destructors, Disruptive Innovators, Beneficiaries, or Casualties will be, we have a pretty good idea of which companies were and are Originators.

Blockchain

We begin with Bitcoin, the brainchild of the enigmatic Satoshi Nakamoto. Bitcoin's introduction of blockchain technology has fundamentally transformed our understanding of digital transactions. This decentralized, transparent ledger system has redefined trust and security, disrupting traditional financial systems. Ethereum has further extended this innovation by introducing smart contracts, enabling decentralized applications (dApps) that run autonomously and securely. Bitcoin opened the door to a new world, and entities like Ethereum and Circle are expanding its horizons, demonstrating the versatility and potential of blockchain technology.

Artificial Intelligence

When it comes to AI, Google DeepMind stands as its first towering figure. The Google-affiliated research lab' achievements, such as AlphaGo, have demonstrated AI's potential in mastering complex tasks previously thought to be the exclusive domain of human intelligence. Not just confined to games, DeepMind's impact encompasses transformative applications in healthcare, energy management, and beyond.

Genomics

In genomics, Illumina has emerged as a transformative force, building on the monumental work of the Human Genome Project (HGP). Completed in 2003, the HGP mapped the entire human genome, providing a comprehensive blueprint of human DNA. This foundational work has revolutionized our understanding of genetics and paved the way for personalized medicine. Illumina has made sequencing the human genome as routine as a blood test, further democratizing access to genetic information. Their technology enables personalized medicine and gene therapy, tailoring treatments to individual genetic profiles.

146

Internet of Things (IoT)

The Internet of Things, a concept introduced by Kevin Ashton, has been brought to life by companies like Cisco. As a leader in networking infrastructure, Cisco has created the backbone for the IoT ecosystem, connecting billions of devices worldwide. This transformation extends from smart homes to industrial automation, fundamentally altering how we live and work. Cisco's IoT solutions exemplify the integration of technology into our daily lives, driving efficiency and innovation across sectors.

Virtual Reality/Augmented Reality

Oculus, under Meta, has been a pioneering force. Oculus transformed VR from a niche technology into a mainstream platform, redefining entertainment, education, and social interaction. The immersive experiences provided by Oculus VR headsets have paved the way for a future where virtual and augmented realities seamlessly blend with our physical world, revolutionizing how we interact with digital environments.

Green Energy

Green energy is no longer a futuristic concept but an urgent necessity, with Tesla leading the way. Tesla revolutionized the automotive industry with electric vehicles and extended its innovation to battery technology, solar energy solutions, and energy storage.

Quantum Computing

Quantum computing is being spearheaded by IBM Quantum. Through the IBM Quantum Experience, IBM is making this cutting-edge technology accessible to researchers and developers. The practical applications of quantum computing in cryptography, materials science, and complex problem-solving are vast and transformative. IBM is turning the theoretical promise of quantum computing into a practical tool with the potential to revolutionize numerous industries.

These pioneering companies are not merely participants in the quantum revolution; they are its architects. Each of these Originators of today's technology revolution have played a critical role in driving the innovations that define our era. They have shattered barriers, expanded the limits of what is possible, and transformed their respective fields. The quantum revolution is not a fleeting trend but a fundamental shift in how we approach technology and its potential to improve our world.

Creative Destructors: The Revolutionaries

Move fast and break things.

—Mark Zuckerberg (Facebook F8 Conference, 2009)

Creative destructors embody Joseph Schumpeter's theory of creative destruction, which posits that the lifeblood of capitalist development is not incremental progress but rather radical innovation that disrupts existing orders, rendering old technologies or business models obsolete. Creative destructors catalyze these profound shifts, introducing innovations that fundamentally reshape industries, redefine consumer expectations, and redraw the competitive landscape.

Creative destructors are more than innovators; they are revolutionaries who do not seek to improve existing systems but to overhaul them entirely. Their role is critical because they not only introduce new technologies but also create the conditions under which these technologies can thrive, often by destroying or fundamentally altering the existing ones. They often see beyond the current applications of a technology to envision transformative uses that challenge and eventually render obsolete the status quo.

By challenging the entrenched norms and introducing more efficient, effective solutions, Creative Destructors not only drive technological adoption but also force entire industries to adapt or die. By breaking down old paradigms, these players clear the path for widespread adoption of new technologies and encourage rapid innovation across industries. This role is crucial in pushing technologies toward maturity—ensuring that they do not just enter the market but come to dominate it, transforming potential into pervasive influence.

Consider the case of Airbnb, which serves as a textbook example of this phenomenon. Airbnb leveraged technology to redefine the lodging industry not by making incremental changes but by completely transforming the concept of what it means to find a place to stay (Hospitality Industry Report, 2024). By turning private homes into potential hotel rooms, Airbnb didn't just offer an alternative to traditional hotels; it challenged and fundamentally changed the norms of the travel industry. It offers a personalized experience that hotels traditionally haven't provided, directly challenging established market leaders.

Disruptive Innovators: The Integrators

If you want something new, you have to stop doing something old.

—Peter Drucker (Innovation and Entrepreneurship, 1985)

That is exactly what Disruptive Innovators offer the technology life cycle. In the context of Clayton Christensen's theory of disruptive innovation, these innovators are the Navy SEALs to tech evolution—elite, precise, and devastatingly effective. They don't simply create new products; they synthesize multiple existing technologies to forge new systems, platforms, or infrastructures. These tech alchemists build on what the Originators crafted and what the disruptors shook up. The result is a new integration of technologies that maximizes utility and accessibility, often transforming entire industries.

By creating complex yet highly functional systems that can be broadly adopted, they enhance efficiency and give rise to new markets. Their knack for melding different technologies into cohesive solutions not only stabilizes these innovations but also standardizes them, thereby fostering the maturation of these technologies.

As described in the previous chapter, Apple is the reigning king of the Disruptive Innovator empire. As the ultimate "second mouse devouring the cheese," Apple has an incredible knack for transforming existing, sometimes clunky, technology into something we can't live without. However, there are other notable examples. Consider the case of Amazon, which has masterfully integrated ecommerce with cloud computing and logistics. This convergence has not only revolutionized retail by transforming the shopping experience but has also reshaped server capacity management for businesses worldwide. Through Amazon Web Services (AWS), Amazon provides scalable cloud computing resources that underpin a vast array of enterprise operations, setting new benchmarks for efficiency and scalability in cloud services.

Similarly, Salesforce has redefined customer relationship management by migrating CRM systems to the cloud. This shift has allowed for scalable, real-time management solutions that profoundly enhance how businesses interact with their customers. Salesforce's cloud-based CRM platform integrates various functionalities—sales, service, and marketing—into a seamless, user-friendly service. This innovation not only improves business efficiency but also elevates the customer experience, pushing the boundaries of what traditional CRM systems can achieve.

Apple, Amazon, and Salesforce didn't just adapt to changes; they redefined the possibilities of existing technology and the industries they've come to dominate, making said technology more accessible and effective. This approach is emblematic of a broader trend in which technology's potential is maximized not just through invention but through clever integration and widespread adoption. As we continue to witness the unfolding of the Quantum Revolution, the impact of these innovators will likely be seen as a pivotal force in shaping the future of technology and business.

Beneficiaries: The Adapters

In Today's era of volatility, there is no other way but to re-invent. The only sustainable advantage you can have over others is agility, that's it. Because nothing else is sustainable, everything else you create, somebody else will replicate.

—Jeff Bezos (Amazon Shareholder Letter, 2015)

While Disruptive Innovators are the sexy, headline-grabbing mavericks of the tech world, there's another group playing a smarter, often more lucrative game: the Beneficiaries. These are the existing giants, the savvy operators who dominate their sectors not by inventing new tech but by exploiting it. Typically positioned adjacent to emerging technologies, Beneficiaries thrive by adopting innovations that complement and enhance their existing operations, products, or services. As these technologies grow, so too do the companies that adeptly integrate them. Beneficiaries ride technology waves all the way up to the top to the maturity phase, creating massive shareholder value as they do.

The companies in this category profit handsomely off of the technologies reaching mass adoption and becoming, yes, boring. These "Barons of Boring" play a vital role in the life cycle of innovation. By integrating new technologies into their workflows, they validate these tools' practicality and versatility, encouraging further investment and fostering widespread trust. This adoption is crucial for the maturity of any technology, helping it transition from novelty to industry standard.

Consider NVIDIA and Zoom. NVIDIA, originally focused on graphics processors for gaming, adeptly pivoted to position its GPUs at the heart of AI research and development. This strategic shift exploited the explosive growth in AI, catapulting NVIDIA to a leadership position within the tech industry. Here, NVIDIA's growth was fueled not by its own inventions but by its ability to align existing strengths with emerging market demands.

Zoom, meanwhile, harnessed existing video conferencing technologies at a pivotal moment—just as global shifts toward remote work exploded, specifically driven by the COVID pandemic. By refining and popularizing this technology with an intuitive interface and reliable performance, Zoom became indispensable in business, education, and personal communications. Zoom's rise illustrates how Beneficiaries can capture and dominate a market segment by adapting and scaling existing technologies to meet timely needs.

Even looking back at Carnegie Steel during the Industrial Revolution sheds light on this archetype. Carnegie did not invent new steel production techniques but leveraged breakthroughs like the Bessemer Process to massively boost production, propelling his company, U.S. Steel, to unprecedented heights and crushing his competition along the way.

In essence, Beneficiaries are not passive observers but active and strategic players in the technological field. They enhance their market position not by inventing new technologies but by effectively integrating and scaling them. As demonstrated by companies like NVIDIA and Zoom, this approach not only facilitates their own growth but also drives the broader acceptance and practical application of new technologies across various sectors. Beneficiaries, therefore, are crucial in ensuring that innovations reach their full potential and become entrenched in our everyday lives. They are the ones who ride the wave of technological growth, ensuring their own expansion as they go.

Beneficiaries are the industry alphas. Some are active and strategic players scanning the horizon for the next big thing to commandeer, while others happen to be at the right place at the right time, thanks to the perfect mix of technology waves and force field factors. Regardless how they get there, successful Beneficiaries integrate it, scale it, and make it indispensable. As demonstrated by behemoths like NVIDIA and Zoom, this strategy isn't just about growth; it's about domination. Beneficiaries harness the currents of technological innovation to ensure they not only stay on top but also dictate the pace and direction of industry evolution, all while lining the pockets of their shareholders with returns that are the envy of the investment world.

Casualties: The Left Behind

Disruptive innovations can hurt, if you are not the one doing the disrupting.

—Clayton Christensen (The Innovator's Dilemma, 1997)

If Beneficiaries make the best out of technology waves and shifts in force field factors, Casualties misread them or ignore them completely. These are companies or industries that fail to adapt to new technologies and market shifts and find that their products or models are replaced by new, more advanced technologies, rendering the old irrelevant and uncompetitive.

While Casualties might seem like mere losers in the technological race, their decline is a critical component of the creative destruction process. It serves as a cautionary tale for other players in the market, emphasizing the need for agility and innovation. The space left by Casualties often provides opportunities for new entrants and ideas, fostering a competitive environment that is necessary for continual technological evolution.

Do you remember Dell computers? Once a leader in the personal computer market, Dell struggled to maintain its position as mobile and cloud computing technologies emerged. The company was slow to respond to these changes, which ultimately affected its market standing.

Similarly, Blackberry, which dominated the early smartphone market, failed to transition to the touch interface and app ecosystem that now define modern smartphones, leading to its decline.

Traditional entities like Barnes & Noble have also faced significant challenges. The rise of digital content consumption and online retail, led by companies like Amazon, left Barnes & Noble struggling to pivot quickly enough to compete. Their hesitation and slow adaptation to these market shifts significantly impacted their business.

The ability to adapt to new paradigms is essential for survival in the tech industry. Companies that fail to evolve become obsolete, while those that embrace change thrive and drive progress. The stories of these Casualties serve as important lessons, underscoring the need for constant innovation and responsiveness to market shifts.

The Fluidity of Roles

If you don't cannibalize yourself, someone else will.

—Steve Jobs (Apple Worldwide Developers Conference, 1997)

In the world of technology, the roles that companies play are far from fixed. These roles—whether as Originators, Creative Destructors, Disruptive Innovators, Beneficiaries, or Casualties—are fluid and continuously evolving. This fluidity is reflective of the very nature of technology itself, which is ceaselessly advancing and reshaping the business landscape. Companies must adapt, shift, and sometimes entirely transform themselves to survive and thrive amid these waves of innovation.

Take IBM, for example. This company has navigated through various roles over its long history. Initially, it played the role of an Originator with its pioneering work in early computing. As the tech ecosystem that it helped to establish grew, IBM became a Beneficiary, capitalizing on the expansive markets it helped create. Recognizing the potential of newer technologies like cloud computing and AI, IBM later embraced the role of a Creative Destructor, actively disrupting its own traditional business models to stay relevant in a rapidly changing digital landscape.

154

Then, there's Nokia, which offers another vivid narrative of role fluidity. Nokia was once at the forefront of mobile technology, dominating the cellphone market as an Originator in the 1990s. But as the mobile landscape transformed with the advent of smartphones, Nokia found itself a Casualty, unable to adapt quickly enough to the pace of innovation set by new entrants. In recent years, Nokia has been making strides to reinvent itself yet again, this time aiming to be a Disruptive Innovator by spearheading developments in 5G technology and network solutions.

Casualties from Within

Not only are corporate roles fluid within the wider ecosystem of technological revolutions, but sometimes, these roles change within a company. Yes, companies can survive a "casualty product" if it's big enough to have more than one product offering and smart enough to make some tough choices.

Even the most innovative and successful companies can face what are known as "casualties" within their product lines or strategic initiatives. These casualties occur when certain products, services, or strategic directions fail to meet expectations, become outdated, or are poorly received by the market. These "casualties" underscore the complex interplay of timing, readiness, and consumer interest that dictates the success or failure of a certain product or technology.

Juggernaut companies like Apple and Meta have faced setbacks with ambitious projects that didn't quite resonate with the market at their time of release.

Consider Apple's foray into augmented and virtual reality with products like the rumored Vision Pro. The AR/VR sectors are notoriously challenging, fraught with high production costs and significant demands on user acceptance and technology integration. Vision Pro did not achieve the expected traction upon release. But instead of signifying a failure of innovation, it was an instance of the market not being fully prepared for such advanced technology. Apple's ability to recognize this and ultimately pulling the plug on the entire project demonstrated foresight and strategic agility. It also leaves the door open for a resurgence when the market conditions—such as infrastructure development and consumer interest—align more favorably.

Similarly, Meta's significant investment in the Metaverse, a bold reimagining of digital interaction through virtual spaces, represented a substantial pivot from its core business. Despite the groundbreaking nature of this venture, the readiness of the market in terms of privacy concerns, user adoption, and technological infrastructure significantly lagged behind the vision. Like Apple, Meta decided to pull back, reflecting a strategic humility and recognition of current market dynamics. Meta's readiness to adapt and potentially reintroduce these technologies later could capitalize on future shifts in consumer behavior and technological advancements.

In both cases, the potential casualties do not necessarily reflect a misstep but rather an acknowledgment that the current technology landscape and consumer ecosystem might not be ready to fully support these innovations. This understanding allows companies like Apple and Meta to pivot and conserve resources, possibly gearing up for a time when the market is more receptive. These isolated instances of "Casualties" within a company can free up resources and capital to create the next big "disruptive innovation."

These stories highlight a fundamental truth in the tech sector: innovation alone isn't enough.

Companies must also possess the foresight and agility to anticipate and react to technological, social, and economic shifts. It's about continuously recalibrating strategies and sometimes undergoing profound transformations to align with or lead the emerging trends. The companies that master this dynamic, ever-changing dance are the ones that shape the future of technology, while those that can't keep up risk fading into obsolescence.

The Dynamic Journey of Technological Evolution

It is not the strongest of the species that survives, nor the most intelligent that survives. It is the one that is the most adaptable to change.

—Charles Darwin

The technology life cycle is not merely a procession of advancing gadgets and software; it's a living drama populated by dynamic corporate actors—Originators, Creative Destructors, Disruptive Innovators, Beneficiaries, and Casualties. Each plays a crucial role in this continuous saga of creation, destruction, and renewal, a cycle that reshapes industries and redefines consumer experiences with each iteration. The essence of this cycle lies not just in the creation of technology but in the competitive and sometimes ruthless environment in which these creations come to life and either thrive or die.

This dynamic interplay of roles provides a more nuanced understanding of the technological zeitgeist, revealing a world where innovation is not just about new gadgets but about the strategic transformations companies undergo to either lead, follow, or get out of the way.

Understanding these shifting roles is crucial not just for predicting which companies will rise or fall but for grasping the broader implications of these shifts on markets and society. It shows us that the technology life cycle is less a linear path and more a vibrant ecosystem of innovation, where the roles of Originator, Destructor, Innovator, and Beneficiary are not fixed but fluid, influenced by external pressures, internal visions, and the unpredictable nature of technological progress.

Thus, we must be mindful that today's pioneers could be tomorrow's casualties, and today's disruptors could be tomorrow's industry standards. The cycle of technological innovation, with all its creative destruction and renewal, does more than drive economic growth and corporate competition; it fundamentally alters how we live, work, and interact. For companies vying to not just survive but thrive, the key lies in their ability to anticipate changes, adapt strategies, and sometimes, to pivot entirely at crucial junctures.

But what does this mean for investors? How can we capitalize on these cycles, identifying the Creative Destructors from the Beneficiaries and the Originators from the Casualties?

Investing successfully in this environment requires more than sharp instincts; it demands a deep understanding of technological trends and the ability to forecast how these trends will evolve. Investors need to identify not only which technologies have the potential to disrupt but also which companies are equipped to adapt and execute their strategies amid these changes. It's about looking beyond the immediate to grasp the broader implications of technological shifts.

Summary

Consider the irony: Facebook, once the poster child of "move fast and break things," now desperately tries to remain relevant in a world it helped create. IBM, the company that made computers household names, had to reinvent itself to avoid becoming obsolete in the very world it pioneered. Even Apple, the master of disruption, quietly kills its own innovations before the market can do it for them.

This is the brutal reality of technological evolution. No position is sacred, no market share guaranteed, and no innovation permanent. The winners aren't necessarily those who create new technologies but those who master the art of corporate metamorphosis—switching roles as fluidly as actors in a repertory company.

CHAPTER 8

Investing in the Quantum Revolution: An Active, Not Passive, Pursuit

The story of the great transition from the Digital Era to the Quantum Revolution is far more nuanced than just the rapid adoption of new tools; it's about the creation of entirely new technological frameworks and possibilities. We're not just updating our old gadgets; innovations like blockchain, AI, and quantum computing are fundamentally altering the rules of the game.

This book is not a "how-to" on investing in early-stage startups or even mature tech behemoths. Rather, it's meant to help investors of all types navigate the complexities of a new technological era that is rapidly progressing but is still young enough to offer immense opportunities for wealth creation. Much like the rise of Netflix during the Digital Revolution, when its IPO offered shares at $15 and a mere $10,000 investment has now turned into a staggering $5 million, these new technologies hold similar wealth-building potential. Netflix didn't just grow because it was a new tool—it redefined how we consume media and created an entirely new ecosystem. The same transformative potential exists today.

© Tal Elyashiv 2025
T. Elyashiv, *Investing in Revolutions*, https://doi.org/10.1007/979-8-8688-1177-7_8

The goal in the previous chapters is to provide you with the full historical, scientific, and practical picture so you can make the right decisions for yourself. Those decisions certainly won't be the same for everyone, but what we do know is that only a few generations in the last half of a millennia have had the opportunity that is presented to us now in this moment of yet another technological revolution.

The sheer volume of technological advancement today can overwhelm even the most knowledgeable investor or entrepreneur. We have unprecedented access to information and sophisticated tools, enabling decisions with a level of precision once unimaginable. But sometimes access without insight can leave investors disoriented.

A spectrum of industry experts, consultants, corporations, and analysts claim to know what's best, offering their own version of vetting and analysis. However, if history has taught us anything, it's that there are no crystal balls and no all-knowing prophets when it comes to predicting market movements. While the Oracle of Omaha and the Dean of Wall Street make it look effortless, they will be the first to admit that discipline, patience, and adaptability are how to navigate uncertainty. The responsibility of filtering data, evaluating critical factors, and applying foresight to make sound investment decisions ultimately rests on your shoulders.

Identifying opportunities to participate in this exciting revolutionary period is an active, not passive, pursuit. It demands an eagle eye for connecting disparate dots, an ability to read between the lines of prevailing narratives, and the vision to peer beyond the present buzz to gauge future implications. It's a journey that calls for perpetual curiosity and a willingness to immerse oneself in the deluge of innovation.

The convergence of giants like blockchain, AI, and quantum computing is not merely disruptive—it's creating a tidal wave of opportunities for those prepared to engage. But navigating this landscape requires more than just knowledge; it demands the acumen to recognize potential before it fully emerges.

This isn't merely about adaptation; it's about strategically investing where the greatest opportunities lie hidden. In a period characterized by rapid technological progress and significant societal impact, understanding the interplay between these forces is essential for anyone aiming not just to survive but to thrive.

But before anything, ask the right questions.

MACROQUESTIONS and Force Field Factors

We may not be able to see the future, but we can look at what's happening right now and try to forecast where that might lead. The following questions are critical to understanding which ideas and/or trends will sustain or fail and what force field factors are responsible.

Historical Forces of Change

1. Which forces have we seen drive change in the past that may be at work again today? Which of these forces may be at work today?

Historical drivers of change are fundamental forces that have repeatedly shaped human society, economies, and the technological landscape throughout history. These drivers often work in tandem, influencing and accelerating each other, and have the potential to reemerge in contemporary contexts, offering insights into future transformations. Understanding these drivers can help us anticipate shifts in global trends, markets, and behaviors. The following sections outline several key historical drivers, along with examples of their past impacts and potential manifestations today.

Technological Innovation

The Industrial Revolution marked a pivotal moment in history, with innovations like the steam engine and mechanized manufacturing reshaping society, economies, and the environment. Fast-forward to the present, we find ourselves at the brink of another transformation. Advances in artificial intelligence, blockchain, and renewable energy technologies are poised to overhaul industries, labor markets, and societal structures in equally profound ways. The potential for these technologies to drive future economic growth and societal progress is immense, mirroring the scale of change experienced during the Industrial Revolution.

Economic Shifts

The Great Depression remains one of the most significant economic events in history, leading to widespread unemployment and catalyzing changes in regulatory landscapes and economic policies. In the modern era, the digital economy and the emergence of the gig economy are similarly redefining the landscape of employment and business models. These shifts suggest potential long-term implications for how work is structured and how economic value is created and distributed, challenging traditional norms and opening up new avenues for economic engagement.

Sociopolitical Movements

The 1960s civil rights movement in the United States brought about crucial legal and societal changes, promoting the rights and freedoms of marginalized communities. Today, movements such as Black Lives Matter and climate activism continue this legacy, driving forward discussions and policy changes around racial justice and environmental sustainability. These contemporary movements demonstrate the enduring power of sociopolitical activism to enact significant changes and address pressing global challenges.

162

Globalization

The Age of Exploration and the subsequent era of colonialism significantly expanded global trade networks, introducing goods, ideas, and cultures to new corners of the world, albeit with mixed consequences including exploitation and inequality. In contrast, today's digital globalization, characterized by the rapid flow of information and digital services, is knitting the world together in novel ways. This digital interconnectedness impacts local cultures, economies, and governance structures, presenting both opportunities and challenges in the globalized world.

Demographic Changes

Following World War II, the baby boom led to substantial population growth, affecting urban development, education systems, and labor markets. Today, demographic shifts are again at the forefront of societal change, with aging populations in developed countries and younger demographics in developing regions posing distinct challenges and opportunities. These demographic trends impact healthcare, employment, and social services, requiring tailored strategies to harness their potential and address their implications.

Environmental Factors

Historical climatic events like the Little Ice Age had significant impacts on agriculture, settlement patterns, and economies. In the current era, climate change stands as a pivotal environmental driver, demanding innovative policy, technology, and global cooperation to mitigate its effects and adapt to emerging realities. The urgency and scale of the climate challenge necessitate a concerted effort to ensure sustainable development and environmental preservation for future generations.

Scientific Breakthroughs

The discovery of antibiotics marked a revolution in medicine, dramatically reducing mortality from bacterial infections and extending human lifespan. Today, we're witnessing comparable breakthroughs in genomics and personalized medicine, which promise to transform healthcare by offering targeted treatments and preventative measures tailored to individual genetic profiles. These scientific advancements hold the potential to further revolutionize healthcare, making treatments more effective and personalized than ever before.

New Sources of Change

2. Have you spotted any new sources or drivers?

When we delve into the question of identifying new sources of change, we're essentially exploring the currents beneath the surface that promise to shape our future. These sources can be broadly categorized into two distinct but interconnected areas: trends and emerging issues. Both are vital in understanding the dynamics of change, offering insights into how the world might evolve in the coming years.

Trends

Trends are patterns of change that have already begun to manifest and can be observed over time. They are like the currents in the ocean, guiding the direction in which society, technology, economy, and culture are moving. Trends often have a more predictable trajectory, allowing businesses, governments, and individuals to plan and adapt accordingly.

- *Remote Work*: The shift toward remote work had been gradually gaining momentum but was dramatically accelerated by the COVID-19 pandemic. This trend has significant implications for urban planning, commercial real estate, technology infrastructure, and work–life balance norms.

- *Sustainable Consumption*: Awareness and concern about environmental issues have led to a trend toward sustainable consumption. This includes increased demand for products with minimal environmental impact, such as plant-based foods, electric vehicles, and sustainable fashion, reshaping industries and consumer behaviors.

Emerging Issues

Emerging issues, on the other hand, are nascent changes that are just beginning to surface. They may not yet have widespread impact or recognition but have the potential to significantly influence the future. Identifying emerging issues requires keen observation and foresight, as they are like seeds that could grow into major forces of change.

- *CRISPR and Genetic Editing*: While still in its early stages, the technology for gene editing has the potential to revolutionize medicine by treating genetic disorders, enhancing crops, and even resurrecting extinct species. The ethical, social, and regulatory implications are vast and largely uncharted.

- *Quantum Computing*: Quantum computing is an emerging issue that could fundamentally alter the landscape of technology, offering computational power far beyond current capabilities. Its potential applications in cryptography, materials science, and complex system modeling are immense but come with significant technical challenges and ethical considerations.

Understanding the distinction between trends and emerging issues helps us navigate the complexities of change. Trends provide a map of the known, guiding immediate strategy and adaptation, while emerging issues represent the unknown, offering both risks and opportunities for innovation and disruption. Together, they form a comprehensive view of the new sources of change, challenging us to think critically about the future and our role in shaping it. By staying informed and adaptable, we can not only anticipate these changes but also leverage them to create a more sustainable, equitable, and prosperous future.

Forces That Prevent Change

3. Are there negative or destructive forces that actively prevent positive change?

In contemplating the dynamics that shape our future, it's equally important to consider not just the forces that propel us forward but also those that might anchor us in place. These impediments to change serve as critical counterbalances to the currents of transformation, influencing the trajectory of societal, technological, and economic evolution. Understanding these stabilities allows us to anticipate resistance points and recalibrate our expectations regarding the pace and direction of change.

Rules and Regulations

Legal frameworks and regulatory guidelines serve as foundational pillars in safeguarding public safety, equity, and environmental integrity within societies. Established by governments and institutions, these rules and regulations are essential in guiding ethical and responsible practices.

However, their protective purpose can inadvertently become a barrier to the swift innovation and adoption of breakthrough technologies or novel practices. A prime example of this dynamic is observed in the regulation of drone technology. In numerous countries, the stringent regulatory environment concerning drones has notably decelerated their integration into commercial delivery services. Regulatory bodies, tasked with navigating complex issues related to privacy, airspace traffic management, and safety, find themselves in a challenging position to balance innovation with these considerations.

Traditions and Cultural Norms

Societal traditions and cultural norms constitute the bedrock of behaviors and expectations, significantly influencing individual and collective identities. These traditions, while offering a sense of continuity and belonging, can also present substantial resistance to new perspectives and ways of living. For instance, the cultural value placed on owning gas-powered vehicles as symbols of status in certain societies poses a significant obstacle to the acceptance and normalization of electric vehicles (EVs). Despite the clear environmental advantages of EVs, this deep-seated cultural preference underscores the complex challenge of shifting societal norms toward more sustainable practices.

Behavior Patterns

Behavior patterns, deeply ingrained through habit or convenience, often prove resistant to change. These established routines and consumer choices are dictated by familiarity and ease, making the transition to new behaviors, even in light of compelling logical or ethical motivations, a daunting task. The pervasive use of single-use plastics illustrates this challenge well. Despite heightened awareness and concern over the detrimental environmental impacts of plastic waste, the convenience and ubiquity of single-use plastics continue to perpetuate consumer reliance on these materials, highlighting the difficulty in altering entrenched consumer behaviors.

Powerful Stakeholders

Entities wielding significant power over markets or societies, including major corporations, government entities, and influential interest groups, play a pivotal role in shaping the direction and pace of change. These powerful stakeholders may resist transformations that pose threats to their established interests or the status quo. The fossil fuel industry provides a stark illustration, having historically opposed robust climate policies and the subsidization of renewable energy initiatives. Through lobbying and other forms of influence, these industries seek to safeguard their economic interests, demonstrating the significant impact that powerful stakeholders can have on the trajectory of societal and technological progress.

The Laws of Physics

The immutable laws of physics represent the ultimate boundary to human endeavor and technological advancement, setting firm limits on what is achievable. These fundamental principles of nature serve as the definitive constraints against which all innovations and explorations are measured. A notable manifestation of this is the speed of light, which governs the maximum speed at which data can be transmitted. This limitation has profound implications for a range of applications, from the achievable speeds of Internet connectivity to the feasibility of interstellar communication, underscoring the inescapable influence of physical laws on the realm of possibility.

Recognizing these impediments to change, or stabilities, enriches our understanding of the complex interplay between forces of innovation and resistance. By acknowledging and analyzing these roadblocks, we can develop more nuanced strategies for navigating change, advocating for progress that is both ambitious and grounded in the realities of societal, technological, and physical constraints. This balanced perspective ensures that our push for the future is informed, resilient, and adaptable to the inevitable frictions encountered along the way.

Experiences of Everyday People

4. How do we observe the lived experiences of people across a diverse range of communities globally?

Understanding the lived experiences and aspirations of everyday people, especially from diverse populations, is a fundamental aspect of building a more inclusive and equitable society. It involves delving deep into the mosaic of human experiences to uncover the rich tapestry of needs, challenges, desires, and hopes that define individual and communal life across various social strata and cultural backgrounds. This endeavor necessitates a broad, inclusive approach to inquiry, inviting voices from all corners of society to share their stories, struggles, and dreams. The lived experiences of individuals provide us with a window into the realities that different people face daily. These experiences are shaped by a multitude of factors including but not limited to socio-economic status, ethnicity, gender, age, and geographical location. They encompass the joys and triumphs as well as the trials and adversities that people navigate, offering insights into the complex interplay between individual agency and structural forces.

For instance, the experiences of a young woman pursuing STEM education in a traditionally male-dominated field can shed light on barriers such as gender bias and the importance of mentorship and supportive communities in overcoming these challenges. Similarly, the journey of a first-generation immigrant family can highlight the nuances of cultural assimilation, the significance of social support networks, and the aspirations for a better life that drive individuals to navigate and surmount the hurdles of displacement and integration.

Asking individuals about the changes they wish to see in the future to enhance their lived experiences is an equally crucial part of this analysis. This forward-looking perspective not only illuminates the gaps and deficiencies in our current societal structures and services but also paves the way for envisioning solutions that are deeply rooted in the actual needs and desires of the people they aim to serve. Whether it's advocating for more accessible healthcare, championing for inclusive education, pushing for environmental justice, or striving for technological innovations that improve quality of life, the aspirations of everyday people serve as a guiding star for policymakers, activists, and innovators alike.

In essence, engaging with the lived experiences and aspirations of diverse populations is not merely an exercise in empathy and understanding; it is a critical step toward crafting a future that is reflective of the collective will and wisdom of humanity. It challenges us to look beyond our assumptions and biases, to listen with open hearts and minds, and to commit to action that bridges the gap between the world as it is and the world as it could be.

MICROQUESTIONS: The WHO, WHAT, WHEN, and WHY of Investing in Revolutions

Asking macroquestions about global forces is essential, but equally important is understanding your personal risk factors—age, financial status, career stage, and personal goals—all of which shape your approach to investing in transformative technologies.

WHO

Are you prepared for potential volatility? Does your investment horizon align with the growth cycles of emerging technologies? These personal factors must be weighed against external market forces to develop a strategy that not only helps you survive but thrive in a rapidly evolving tech landscape. By balancing internal risk considerations with the opportunities presented by these technological shifts, you can turn disruptions into avenues for advancement.

Understanding Personal Risk Tolerance and Capacity:

Investing in revolutionary technologies like AI and blockchain offers exciting potential but comes with significant risks. Investors need to assess not only the rewards but also how much financial and emotional risk they can handle. Risk tolerance refers to how comfortable you are with uncertainty and potential losses, while risk capacity measures how much risk you can financially afford. Balancing these two factors is key.

For instance, if you have short-term goals, such as saving for a home, investing in early and volatile technology segments like AI technology may be too risky, as the short-term fluctuations might not give you time to recover from downturns. On the other hand, with long-term goals like retirement, you can afford to ride out market volatility, making higher-risk, high-reward investments more feasible, at least with portions of your investment portfolio.

Financial Wherewithal and Investment Decisions:

The amount of money an investor can comfortably risk also plays a major role in their strategy. For someone with a smaller net worth, a significant loss could jeopardize their financial security, while someone with substantial assets may be able to absorb losses more easily. This difference in risk capacity should drive decisions related to the investments amounts allocated to more risky and volatile investments.

WHAT

Once you've assessed your personal risk factors, the next step is determining which industry sectors and subdomains you want to invest in. The convergence of AI, quantum computing, and blockchain will profoundly impact numerous industries, making it critical to identify sectors most likely to benefit from these innovations. For example:

- *Healthcare/Medicine:* AI and quantum computing are transforming healthcare with personalized medicine, faster drug discovery, and predictive analytics for patient care. Blockchain can improve data security and transparency in medical records, opening up vast opportunities for innovation in the healthcare sector.

- *Manufacturing:* Quantum computing promises to revolutionize manufacturing by optimizing supply chains and production processes with unprecedented speed and accuracy. AI-driven automation is already reshaping the industry, improving efficiency, and reducing costs.

- *Warfare/Defense:* The defense sector is increasingly reliant on AI for real-time data analysis, autonomous systems, and predictive modeling in conflict zones. Quantum computing's potential to break encryption could also redefine cybersecurity, making it a critical area of investment.

Understanding how these technologies will disrupt key industries empowers you to make strategic investment choices. While AI is already delivering immediate advancements in healthcare, improving diagnostics and patient care, quantum computing holds the potential to revolutionize industries like logistics, energy, and finance, though its

172

full impact may take longer to materialize. By focusing on sectors most likely to be transformed by the Quantum Revolution, you can position your investments for significant, long-term growth. This approach allows you not just to participate in the evolution of these industries but to fully capitalize on the profound shifts that will define the future.

WHO: The Players

Navigating the quantum revolution requires understanding the different roles companies play within this ever-evolving ecosystem. Each category of company presents unique investment opportunities and challenges, shaped by where they stand in the technology life cycle. Recognizing these categories—and their associated risk and reward profiles—can help investors develop strategies that balance risk and maximize returns.

Originators: High Risk/High Reward

At the cutting edge of innovation, Originators are the pioneers developing new, unproven technologies. These companies operate in the early stages of the technology life cycle, where risks are significant—ranging from regulatory hurdles to market adoption uncertainties. However, the potential rewards are equally high. If successful, Originators can disrupt entire industries and capture significant market share. Investing in these companies requires a high tolerance for uncertainty but offers the chance to be part of a transformative breakthrough.

Creative Destructors: Medium to High Risk/ High Reward

Creative Destructors use existing, validated technologies to disrupt established business models. They don't need to invent new technology from scratch but focus on applying innovations in ways that challenge industry norms. The risk here is lower than for Originators, as the technology is already proven, but the challenge lies in overcoming competitive pushback and market inertia. Investors in Creative Destructors can benefit from significant growth as these companies force traditional players to adapt or be left behind.

Disruptive Innovators: High Risk/Very High Reward

Disruptive Innovators often start in niche markets, operating with high uncertainty but massive potential. These companies seek to redefine entire industries, though scalability and market validation remain significant hurdles. The risk is high, as not all disruptors succeed in reaching mainstream adoption. However, when they do, the rewards can be enormous, with the potential to completely reshape sectors. Investors who can identify these companies early may see exceptional returns, but only if the innovators overcome their obstacles.

Beneficiaries: Low to Medium Risk/Medium to High Reward

Beneficiaries are established companies that integrate new technologies to enhance their operations. They aren't developing the technology but using it to improve efficiency, gain competitive advantages, and solidify their market positions. The risks are generally lower, focused on successful implementation rather than invention. When these companies integrate new technologies effectively, they can achieve significant cost savings and growth, offering investors reliable, if somewhat less dramatic, returns.

Casualties: Very High Risk/Low Reward

Finally, there are the Casualties—companies that fail to adapt to technological change and find themselves in decline. Unable to keep pace with innovation, these businesses face shrinking market share, declining revenues, and the threat of obsolescence. For investors, these companies

174

present high risk with limited upside, often requiring restructuring or even facing bankruptcy. Avoiding these companies—or identifying them early enough to exit—can save investors from significant losses.

HOW: The Pathways (Strategies and Investment Methods)

Investing in disruptive technologies offers a broad array of opportunities, from high-risk venture capital plays to more stable dividend growth and defensive strategies. The key to success lies in understanding the unique characteristics of each investment method, its risks and rewards, and how it fits into the evolving landscape of technological transformation. Let's explore some of the key methods investors use to participate in these technological revolutions.

Early-Stage Investments: High Risk, High Reward

For those who are willing to embrace the uncertainty of breakthrough innovations, early-stage investments offer access to companies at the cutting edge of technological development.

- *Venture capital* is a popular choice for institutional investors, with staged financing allowing capital to be deployed incrementally as startups achieve key milestones. Although this structure helps manage risk, early-stage companies face high failure rates and long investment horizons. The upside, however, can be transformative: investors can see massive returns if a startup successfully brings its technology to market.

- *Angel investing* presents a similar opportunity, but with a personal twist. Individual investors provide seed capital directly to promising startups. The personal nature of these investments comes with high risk, as early-stage startups often struggle with market fit and scalability. Yet, the potential for outsized returns remains a powerful incentive.

- *Equity crowdfunding* platforms like Kickstarter and Indiegogo have opened the door for smaller investors to get involved in early-stage companies, democratizing access to startup equity. The risks are considerable, but the accessibility of these platforms allows investors to spread their capital across multiple ventures, reducing exposure to any single project.

Growth Equity: Medium Risk, High Reward

As companies move beyond the startup phase and start scaling, growth equity strategies become more attractive. Investors can target companies that have already demonstrated market viability but still have considerable room for expansion.

- *Growth equity funds* focus on companies showing strong market adoption and revenue growth, offering a balance between risk and reward. These companies have moved past the highest-risk phase but are still scaling, which can lead to volatility. Nonetheless, the upside potential remains significant as they continue to capture market share.

- *Thematic ETFs* provide an accessible way to diversify without picking individual stocks and gain exposure to high-growth sectors like AI, robotics, and quantum computing. For instance, the iShares Robotics and Artificial Intelligence ETF (IRBO) allows investors to tap into a portfolio of companies within the AI ecosystem.

Sector-specific ETFs can still be volatile, especially in emerging technology fields, but they provide a way to spread risk across multiple companies, reducing the exposure to a single entity's failure.

- *Commodities and Technology-Linked Materials:* As technologies like electric vehicles (EVs), AI, and quantum computing evolve, the demand for specific commodities such as lithium (for batteries), cobalt, and rare earth metals continues to grow. These materials are essential for the production of these new technologies.

Investing in commodities or commodity-focused ETFs allows investors to gain exposure to these critical materials. However, commodities can be highly volatile, with prices influenced by global supply chain disruptions, geopolitical tensions, and environmental regulations. Despite these risks, commodities offer an indirect way to benefit from technological advancements and can also serve as a hedge against inflation. By tapping into the demand for key resources, investors can position themselves to capitalize on the growth of emerging technologies.

Mature Companies: Lower Risk, Steady Returns

As technologies mature, investors may shift their focus to established companies that have successfully integrated these innovations into their business models.

- *Blue-chip stocks* represent large, well-established firms that have adapted to technological changes and maintained strong market positions. These companies offer lower growth potential compared to high-risk startups, but they provide steady returns, making them suitable for long-term, conservative portfolios.

- *Dividend growth stocks* offer investors income by looking to companies that consistently generate profits and share them with shareholders. These firms may not lead the next wave of technological innovation, but they can reap the rewards by adopting new technologies to enhance their operations. Dividend-paying stocks offer the benefit of regular income and the potential for capital appreciation over time, with risks tied primarily to how effectively these companies implement new technologies.

Tailored Risk Management: Private Equity and Hedge Funds

For more sophisticated investors, private equity and hedge funds provide additional pathways to navigate technological revolutions.

- *Private equity* focuses on companies that are not yet publicly traded but are poised for growth. These investments offer the potential for high returns, especially when companies are gearing up for public offerings or acquisitions. However, private equity is often illiquid, with long lockup periods making it difficult to exit before a company matures.

- *Hedge funds* offer more flexibility by using advanced strategies like long/short positions, derivatives, and arbitrage to maximize returns or minimize risks. Hedge funds may invest in both public and private companies, allowing them to hedge against market volatility while targeting high-growth opportunities. While hedge funds can deliver strong returns in turbulent markets, they come with high fees and the potential for significant losses if market bets don't pay off.

Defensive Strategies: Protecting Against Decline

Not all companies will adapt to technological disruption successfully. When investing in companies at risk of becoming Casualties, defensive strategies like short selling and put options come into play.

- *Short selling* allows investors to profit from a company's declining stock price by borrowing shares, selling them, and repurchasing them at a lower price. This strategy is risky, as losses can be unlimited if the stock price unexpectedly rises, but it can be highly profitable for investors who accurately predict a company's downfall.

- *Put options* offer a more controlled way to hedge against potential losses. Investors purchase the right to sell a stock at a predetermined price, protecting themselves from sharp declines. While the cost of the option may be lost if the stock price doesn't drop, put options limit the downside risk and help safeguard portfolios during times of market disruption.

Building a Balanced Strategy

The rapidly evolving world of disruptive technologies presents a wide range of investment methods, from high-risk early-stage ventures to more stable plays in mature companies and defensive strategies to protect against market downturns. A well-rounded approach combines exposure to high-growth areas like venture capital and thematic ETFs with the stability of blue-chip stocks and dividend payers. By choosing the right blend of methods, investors can not only participate in technological revolutions but also protect their portfolios from the inevitable risks of innovation.

The Pitfall of a "One Trick Pony" Strategy

Investors often make the mistake of focusing on a single industry or company that shows promise due to emerging trends or rapid growth. While this may offer short-term gains, it carries significant risks by ignoring the fast-evolving nature of markets and the broader impact of technological convergence.

True breakthroughs rarely happen within a single field. Instead, innovation thrives at the intersection of multiple technologies, where synergies create exponential growth and new possibilities. For example, blockchain's secure and transparent infrastructure has the potential to revolutionize various industries, but it's the integration of AI—through advanced data processing, pattern recognition, and intelligent decision-making—that unlocks its full potential.

The most effective investment strategies recognize that the future lies in the convergence of technologies. Companies that embrace multiple innovations, creating synergies across fields, are positioned for long-term success. Leaders like NVIDIA, AMD, Apple, Microsoft, and Alphabet have capitalized on this by integrating technologies like AI and blockchain to diversify their offerings and drive growth.

Amazon leverages the convergence of technology in a uniquely extraordinary way: through a cohesive strategy that integrates innovations across various sectors. By combining advancements in cloud computing, AI, automation, and data analytics, Amazon has created a synergistic ecosystem that drives both operational efficiency and market expansion.

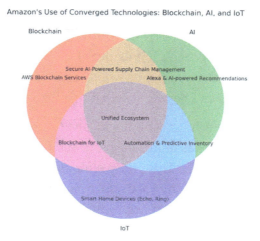

Figure 8-1. Investment Ecosystem in the Quantum Revolution. It maps out four quadrants: Originators, Creative Destructors, Beneficiaries, and Casualties. The diagram emphasizes diversification across sectors, showing how convergence among technologies like blockchain, AI, and quantum computing drives opportunities

Investing in the quantum revolution requires a clear understanding of how companies fit within the larger innovation ecosystem. Diversifying investments across sectors and technologies helps mitigate risk while tapping into the transformative power of convergence. Investors should actively monitor technological trends and market shifts, adjusting their strategies to stay ahead in this rapidly evolving landscape.

WHEN: Timing Is Everything

Timing investments in technology requires an understanding of technology life cycles, which is crucial for predicting technology adoption and market saturation points. Each phase of a technology's life cycle—from inception and early adoption to mainstream acceptance and eventual decline—presents unique opportunities and risks:

- *Early Adoption Phase:* Investing during this phase can be highly risky but also offer substantial rewards if the technology succeeds. It is essential for investors to recognize inflection points where a technology proves its potential and begins to gain market traction.

- *Growth Phase:* As a technology moves into the growth phase, it becomes more accepted, and the market for it expands rapidly. This phase often offers the most lucrative opportunities for returns on investment as the technology begins to reach its full market potential.

- *Maturity and Decline:* Eventually, all technologies face saturation; new innovations may make earlier ones obsolete. Successful investors monitor emerging trends to anticipate these shifts and reallocate investments to newer technologies before returns diminish.

Too Early, Too Late, or Just Plain Wrong

Timing is not everything, but it's a lot. The evolution of revolutionary technologies presents a conundrum: invest too early, too late, or in the wrong technology, and the consequences can be costly, both in missed opportunities and squandered resources. Understanding these dynamics through the lens of past and present examples illuminates the delicate art of timing in technology adoption and investment.

The Peril of Too Early: Investing in technology before the market is ready can be as perilous as it is visionary. Consider the tale of General Magic, a company that in the early 1990s developed a handheld communication device essentially akin to today's smartphones. It featured touchscreens, Internet connectivity, and portable computing—decades before Apple or Samsung capitalized on these technologies. General

Magic's vision was revolutionary, but the world wasn't ready. The necessary infrastructure, including widespread Internet access and robust mobile networks, was not in place. Consumers were also not primed for such a device, leading to its commercial failure. The company was too early, and by the time the rest of the world caught up, others were ready to capitalize on the groundwork General Magic had laid.

Too Hyped and Overpriced: When a technology reaches the height of its hype, investor enthusiasm and media attention can push valuations far beyond the technology's actual readiness or proven market potential, leading to the creation of a "pricing bubble." In this phase, the market becomes overly optimistic, and the gap between expectations and reality widens. Investors pour in capital, expecting rapid growth and returns, but the underlying technology may not yet be mature or commercially viable. This disconnect often leads to a market correction, with significant losses for those who invested at the height of the hype.

Take Initial Coin Offerings (ICOs) in 2017. While blockchain technology has legitimate and promising applications, the rapid rise of hundreds of new digital currencies, fueled by speculative investment and media hype, led to a bubble. Many ICOs were launched without solid business models or working products, causing the bubble to burst as regulatory scrutiny increased and investors began to lose confidence.

Similarly, in emerging fields like quantum computing, there is growing concern that hype may outpace actual progress. While these technologies hold incredible potential, the timeline for commercial viability and widespread adoption remains unclear. Investors who jump in too early, driven by inflated expectations, risk being caught in a speculative bubble, where the promise has yet to materialize in practical applications.

The Danger of Too Late: Technology is in the decline phase. Conversely, entering the market too late can leave companies scrambling to catch up with established players, often at a significant disadvantage. BlackBerry's response to the iPhone serves as a cautionary tale. Once a leader in the smartphone market, BlackBerry underestimated the shift toward touchscreens and app-based ecosystems, clinging instead to its keyboards and email-focused devices. By the time BlackBerry acknowledged its mistake, Apple and Android had dominated the new landscape. BlackBerry's delay in adopting the new technology paradigms cost it its leadership position, relegating it to a minor player in the market it once led.

The Risk of the Wrong Technology: Choosing the wrong technology— even if the timing is right—can lead organizations down a costly path of obsolescence. Take the battle of HD DVD versus Blu-ray in the mid-2000s. Toshiba's HD DVD and Sony's Blu-ray were competing formats for high-definition video. Despite considerable investment and industry support, HD DVD lost to Blu-ray, which offered greater storage capacity and had better industry backing, including prominent film studios. Toshiba's bet on HD DVD was not necessarily poorly timed but was the wrong technology to back, leading to significant financial losses and missed market opportunities.

The lessons from past technological inflections teach us that success in innovation is not merely about creating or funding breakthrough technologies but also about understanding the ecosystem in which these technologies will operate. It requires a keen sense of timing, an understanding of market readiness, and an ability to pivot away from the wrong technologies—even if they are beloved or well-funded. Navigating the complex landscape of technological innovation requires not just vision but a deep understanding of the many factors that contribute to a technology reaching its tipping point. For investors and innovators alike, the history of technology offers not just cautionary tales but a road map for navigating future revolutions.

Summary

So you've asked the right questions and understand the answers. You've done your homework, educating yourself about the technology, the companies, and the various investment tools at your disposal. You've also developed a keen understanding of your own financial landscape— your time horizons, risk tolerance, and areas of interest. You're ready to make a move.

In the next chapter, we'll outline investment scenarios and the considerations for investing in three specific markets where we know the Quantum Revolution's transformation technologies will converge and innovate in radical ways. We'll explore the "Who, What, When, Where, and How" in the healthcare, defense, and manufacturing verticals so you can conceptualize how to transform the knowledge you've gained from previous chapters and put it into practice.

The opportunities for wealth creation are there for the taking, but they require a proactive approach and strategic thinking. Investing in these markets (and so many others) isn't just about tapping into new technologies; it's about understanding their potential to disrupt and redefine the future.

Each market presents its own set of challenges and rewards, so it's crucial to remain vigilant and adaptable. The pace of change will be swift in some areas and painfully slow in others. An investment that looks promising today might need reassessment tomorrow as new technologies emerge and market dynamics shift.

Throughout the previous chapters, I've attempted to equip you with knowledge to analyze and possibly foresee any number of scenarios that may come to fruition in the months and years to come. By the end of the next chapter, you'll have a solid foundation to apply your knowledge strategically and make investment choices that not only align with your financial goals but also position you at the forefront of innovation—seizing the opportunities that the Quantum Revolution has to offer.

CHAPTER 9

Quantum Revolution Investment Scenario Examples, or Putting Theory to Practice

Transformative technologies are driving unprecedented opportunities—not just for industries but for investors who understand the moment. Think about it: At the dawn of every major technological revolution, there were those who saw the writing on the wall before anyone else. They were the ones who invested not just in companies, but in ideas, movements, and ecosystems that would come to define the future. The Industrial Revolution didn't make a few people rich because they bet on better steam engines; it made them rich because they understood that the entire fabric of the economy was about to change. We're there again—except this time, it's not just one technology; it's a convergence of them.

In the late 1990s, few people fully grasped what the Internet would become. But those who did weren't just betting on faster email systems—they were building and investing in platforms that would transform how we shop, communicate, and do business. They recognized that technology wasn't just a tool but the foundation for a new era of wealth creation.

© Tal Elyashiv 2025
T. Elyashiv, *Investing in Revolutions*, https://doi.org/10.1007/979-8-8688-1177-7_9

Today, we're at the threshold of a similar revolution. AI, quantum computing, and blockchain's foundational shifts will redefine entire industries—from healthcare and finance to defense and manufacturing. For the investor, this isn't about picking one or two winners; it's about seeing the entire landscape and understanding how these technologies converge, multiply, and ultimately reshape the economy.

But this isn't a prediction at all. What we're talking about here is a broad range of scenarios that are grounded in the insights gained throughout this book. The aim is not to forecast a single outcome but to illuminate how transformational technologies will shape the future across many possible paths.

The world today is again at a crossroads. By 2030, AI alone is projected to contribute over $15 trillion to the global economy. Blockchain is poised to overhaul everything from banking to supply chains, with potential applications expected to reach $3.1 trillion (McKinsey Global Institute, 2023). Quantum computing, once confined to the theoretical, is starting to revolutionize drug discovery, cybersecurity, and financial modeling at a scale that could dwarf what we've seen before.

But the real opportunity isn't just in these technologies individually. It's in how they're converging to create entirely new ecosystems. In healthcare, AI is turning predictive diagnostics into a reality, while quantum computing accelerates drug discovery. In manufacturing, blockchain is ensuring end-to-end transparency, while the Internet of Things (IoT) enables fully autonomous, smart factories. And in defense, autonomous drones powered by AI are already reshaping battlefield dynamics. What's clear is that the smart money won't be on the technologies themselves but on the companies and sectors that figure out how to leverage them in tandem.

Now, I want to make something very clear: This chapter does not include investment advice in any specific company or financial instrument. It is merely a demonstration of how the concepts discussed in the book can be deployed to drive better investment decisions regarding transformational technologies. The aim is to provide a framework for understanding how these technologies could reshape industries, not to tell you which stocks to buy.

So, how do you invest in this future? You don't just bet on one breakthrough—you recognize the broad shifts and position yourself accordingly. This means identifying the players who are building the platforms, the infrastructure, and the ecosystems that will power the next wave of growth while simultaneously becoming master of the universe of force-field factors around you.

The lesson from history is clear: The biggest investment opportunities arise when the fabric of the economy shifts, when new technologies don't just enhance what already exists but create entirely new markets, and when society as a whole is primed for the revolution. We've seen it with railroads, with electricity, with the Internet—and now, we're seeing it with the convergence of AI, quantum computing, blockchain, and beyond. The question is: will you be one of the people who reads the writing on the wall?

EXAMPLE 1: Defense and Warfare in the Quantum Revolution

WHY: Setting the Force Field Factor Stage

The world is entering a new era of heightened geopolitical tension, where the decades-long "holiday from history" has come to an end. Conflicts that were once considered unlikely or distant are now defining the global landscape. The Russia–Ukraine war, China's ambitions in Taiwan, and rising tensions in the Middle East involving Iran, Hamas, the Houthis, and Hezbollah are all contributing to an increasingly volatile environment. Meanwhile, military posturing between North Korea, the United States,

South Korea, and Japan continues to simmer. As these conflicts escalate, military spending is surging worldwide, with nations scrambling to modernize their defense systems and prepare for future warfare scenarios.

Not surprisingly, total global military expenditure reached $2443 billion in 2023, an increase of 6.8% in real terms from 2022. This was the steepest year-on-year increase since 2009. The ten largest spenders in 2023—led by the United States, China, and Russia—all increased their military spending, according to data on global military spending published by the Stockholm International Peace Research Institute (SIPRI, 2023).

According to Nan Tian, Senior Researcher with SIPRI's Military Expenditure and Arms Production Programme, "The unprecedented rise in military spending is a direct response to the global deterioration in peace and security."

While unsettling, the geopolitical uncertainty (at best) and heating up (at worst) is a massive force field factor that is proving to be a powerful catalyst for and accelerant in the usage of today's most advanced technologies.

Technologies Converge in the Battlefield

The nature of modern warfare is changing rapidly, driven by advanced technologies like artificial intelligence (AI), autonomous systems, and quantum computing. Gone are the days of traditional battlefield engagements; now, warfare is conducted through drone swarms, real-time AI-driven decision-making, and cyberattacks that can cripple entire defense infrastructures. These technologies are not only disrupting the defense industry but are also creating unprecedented investment opportunities.

What we are witnessing across these conflicts is not just the adoption of individual technologies like AI or autonomous robotics but the convergence of these technologies in ways that are transforming warfare as we know it. The use of drones, for instance, is becoming more sophisticated as AI is integrated to enhance autonomy and decision-making. These AI-driven systems can work in tandem with quantum encryption to ensure secure communications and prevent cyberattacks.

This convergence is being driven by the increasing unpredictability of global geopolitics. The heightened tensions in regions like Eastern Europe and the Middle East are accelerating the deployment of these advanced technologies. Militaries are under immense pressure to innovate and adopt new systems that allow for faster, more accurate decision-making, enhanced situational awareness, and greater operational efficiency. As a result, we are seeing technologies that were once confined to research labs now being operationalized in the battlefield.

The rapid evolution of modern warfare technologies is not just a glimpse of the future but a reality unfolding today. Drones and AI-driven systems are no longer experimental; they are critical components of active military strategies. As the geopolitical landscape continues to shift, the adoption and convergence of these technologies will only accelerate, reshaping the nature of warfare and creating new investment opportunities in the defense and technology sectors.

Ukraine: A Quantum Revolution Inflection Point

The Russia–Ukraine war is a prime example of how modern conflict is being reshaped by cutting-edge technology, and Ukraine has become a testing ground for some of the most advanced military applications, with technologies like drones, AI, and augmented/virtual reality (AR/VR) being integrated into their defensive and offensive strategies.

Startups and tech companies have supplied Ukraine with AI-powered surveillance systems, autonomous drones, and data analytics platforms that allow the country to react swiftly and efficiently to battlefield developments. Companies like Palantir, NVIDIA, and Applied Intuition are working closely with governments to develop AI platforms capable of automating complex tasks, from threat detection to operational planning.

"The long and the short of it is: Behaviors are changing," according to Jason Brown, Applied Intuition Defense's general manager, "There's no comparison between what existed before 1995, let's say, and today."

"Software and data are now, really, the weapons that matter most," he said. "A lot of people don't consider them weapons, but I think that's shortsighted."

By providing these cutting-edge tools, the private sector is not only enabling military forces to act faster but also making them more efficient, with AI assisting in decisions that would have taken hours or days using traditional methods.

This war has demonstrated the effectiveness of private sector technology in real-time conflict and how essential it has become in modern defense strategies. The rapid deployment and adaptation of tech-driven solutions in Ukraine has provided a template for how governments and the private sector can collaborate to address evolving military needs.

AI and Data Processing: Strategic Edge for Ukraine

Ukraine has been utilizing AI to enhance battlefield decision-making by processing vast amounts of data from drones, satellite imagery, and intelligence reports. AI-driven systems provide real-time battlefield analysis and predictive insights, allowing Ukrainian forces to anticipate Russian troop movements and make faster, more informed strategic decisions. AI also automates targeting systems, enabling quicker and more precise strikes, and plays a critical role in intercepting and disrupting Russian communications.

Drone Warfare: Autonomous and Effective

Drones have become essential in Ukraine's military strategy, with both sides using them for reconnaissance and attacks. Ukraine has advanced this with AI-powered autonomous drone swarms, which communicate and adapt in real time with minimal human intervention. These drones, capable of coordinated attacks and surveillance, are redefining modern warfare. Ukraine has also modified commercial drones for military use, deploying them effectively in urban and complex environments.

AR/VR: Enhancing Training and Combat Awareness

Ukrainian forces are leveraging augmented reality (AR) for enhanced situational awareness, with real-time data overlays that show enemy positions and mission objectives directly in soldiers' views. Virtual reality (VR) is used for immersive training, allowing soldiers to rehearse missions and battlefield scenarios, preparing them for high-stakes engagements without real-world risks.

WHO: Key Players in Defense Innovation

The defense industry is now characterized by a mix of large, established defense contractors and nimble tech startups. Understanding this spectrum is crucial for investors looking to navigate the opportunities in the space:

- *Large Defense Contractors (Incumbents):* Companies like Lockheed Martin, Northrop Grumman, Raytheon Technologies (RTX), General Dynamics, BAE Systems, and Boeing continue to dominate traditional defense systems like aircraft, tanks, and missile systems. These firms are essential for massive, long-term military projects that require stability and high-dollar government contracts. They are now expanding into emerging technologies to stay competitive.

- *Disruptive Tech companies (Dual-Use Companies):* Newer players like Anduril Industries, Palantir Technologies, SpaceX, Shield AI, Capella Space, and Epirus are leading the charge in AI, autonomy, and space-based defense solutions. Many of these companies offer dual-use technologies, serving both commercial markets and defense applications. For instance, Palantir is revolutionizing battlefield data processing, as well as assisting commercial and civil government sectors with big data analytics, and Anduril is advancing autonomous combat drones.

- *Private Sector Innovators:* Companies like Applied Intuition, Scale AI, and Shield AI are bridging the gap between defense and commercial applications, building advanced AI software, and real-time battlefield data analytics. These private sector firms are creating solutions faster than traditional defense contractors, making them attractive to military buyers looking for agility and innovation.

WHAT: Key Technologies Driving the Defense Revolution

The future of defense lies in the convergence of several key technologies:

- *AI and Autonomy:* AI is transforming decision-making on the battlefield, with predictive analytics, automated targeting systems, and real-time battlefield intelligence. Autonomous systems, such as drones, unmanned ground vehicles, and marine vessels, are being deployed to conduct surveillance, reconnaissance, and combat operations with minimal human intervention.

- *Cybersecurity and Space:* As warfare shifts to include
  space and cyberspace, defense companies like SpaceX
  and Capella Space are launching satellite networks for
  surveillance and defense operations. Cybersecurity
  solutions are becoming increasingly critical, as state
  actors seek to compromise defense systems through
  cyberattacks.

- *Directed Energy and Quantum Computing:* Companies
  like Epirus are developing directed-energy weapons,
  such as antidrone systems, while quantum computing
  is starting to be integrated into secure communications
  and encryption for military applications.

WHEN: Timing-Related Consideration

- *Now*: The defense technology market is entering a
  critical phase, where many innovations are moving
  from R&D into operational deployment. AI-driven
  systems, autonomous drones, and advanced
  surveillance satellites are already playing active roles in
  modern conflicts.

- *Next 5–10 Years (and Beyond)*: AI, blockchain,
  and quantum computing technologies, though
  still emerging, will gain more traction as critical
  components for secure communications, logistics,
  and intelligence. Investors looking to benefit from this
  trend should consider early-stage investments in firms
  developing these capabilities.

HOW: Investment Strategies

There are a variety possible strategies investors can employ to capitalize on the technology revolution in defense. Here, we outline just a few:

- *Diversify Across Established and Emerging Players (Disruptive Innovators)*: A balanced approach involves investing in large defense contractors like Lockheed Martin or Northrop Grumman for stability while also backing high-growth, riskier startups such as Anduril, Shield AI, or Epirus that are disrupting the market with new technologies.

- *Focus on Dual-Use Technologies*: Companies that serve both commercial and defense markets offer the most promise. Firms like SpaceX (commercial space travel and military satellite launches) and Palantir (enterprise data analytics and battlefield intelligence) have the flexibility to serve multiple sectors, enhancing their growth potential.

- *Follow Government Contracts, Adoption, and Financial Inflection Points*: Watch for which companies win major defense contracts or land government partnerships. For example, Anduril's selection by the US Air Force to develop collaborative combat aircraft or Palantir's $480 million Army contract may be clear indicators of future growth.

- *Invest in Technology Enablers (Originators)*: Companies developing key enabling technologies like AI (e.g., Scale AI), autonomous systems, and cybersecurity (e.g., Shield AI) are likely to see rapid growth as defense departments worldwide adopt these innovations.

EXAMPLE 2: Healthcare in the Quantum Revolution

WHY: Setting the Force Field Factor Stage

Imagine a future where healthcare is predictive rather than reactive and treatments are as personalized as your DNA sequence. AI-driven diagnostic tools analyze your genome, lifestyle, and real-time health data collected by IoT devices, generating a personalized health plan tailored just for you. As Eric Topol, a leading voice in digital health, said, "The future of medicine is data-driven, with the ability to predict and prevent diseases before they manifest." Technologies like quantum computing could dramatically accelerate the development of new drugs by simulating molecular interactions with unprecedented speed and accuracy, while blockchain ensures that your personal medical data remains secure, accessible only to authorized healthcare providers.

The world is experiencing a profound shift in healthcare, driven by rapid advancements in technology and a global imperative to improve healthcare systems amid growing demands. A 2022 report by Deloitte highlights that global healthcare systems are facing "a perfect storm" of challenges, including aging populations, rising chronic diseases, and overburdened healthcare infrastructures. As the report emphasizes, the need to "do more with less" is pushing healthcare providers to adopt innovative technologies that can deliver higher-quality care more efficiently.

Take the case of the Cleveland Clinic, one of the pioneers in leveraging AI for predictive healthcare. Tom Mihaljevic, CEO of Cleveland Clinic, said, "AI will be the cornerstone of predictive medicine in the future. We've already seen AI-assisted algorithms outperform humans in diagnosing diseases like breast cancer and lung cancer." In a groundbreaking study, AI accurately predicted the onset of heart disease five years earlier than traditional diagnostic tools, offering a glimpse into the future of predictive healthcare.

Healthcare systems are undergoing a transformation, leveraging cutting-edge innovations to redefine the delivery and quality of care. According to the World Health Organization, by 2030, global healthcare demand will grow by 50%, primarily due to the rise in chronic diseases and aging populations. This is pushing healthcare providers to not only adopt new technologies but also rethink how care is delivered, making AI, telemedicine, robotics, and genomics central to modern healthcare.

In 2023, global healthcare spending reached unprecedented levels, driven by the lasting impacts of the COVID-19 pandemic and the ongoing demand for more robust public health infrastructures. Global healthcare spending is expected to reach $10 trillion by 2026, according to a report from PwC, with much of this investment focused on AI, genomics, telemedicine, and other advanced technologies. Governments and private sectors alike are pouring billions into healthcare innovation—not just to respond to immediate crises but to lay the groundwork for long-term improvements in care delivery. For example, the US government alone allocated $500 million in 2023 for AI-driven research in healthcare, aiming to enhance early diagnosis and preventive care.

As geopolitical instability drives military spending, healthcare is experiencing a similar acceleration in technology adoption—though in response to societal rather than political pressures. The need to deliver faster, more personalized, and accessible healthcare is creating a "force field effect," rapidly propelling healthcare technology to the forefront of global priorities. This is especially evident in the rise of telemedicine, which saw a 1,000% increase in usage during the COVID-19 pandemic, and is now a permanent fixture in healthcare systems worldwide. Dr. Vivian Lee, President of Health Platforms at Verily, remarked, "Telemedicine is not just a stopgap solution. It's the future of healthcare delivery, enabling more people to access care regardless of geography."

Healthcare's Technological Renaissance

The healthcare sector is in the midst of a profound transformation, driven by the convergence of advanced technologies and accelerated by global crises like COVID-19. Just as geopolitical uncertainty is catalyzing military innovation, societal pressures such as aging populations, chronic diseases, and future pandemics are accelerating healthcare innovation.

With AI, genomics, telemedicine, and robotics leading the way, the future of healthcare is becoming increasingly personalized, data-driven, and patient-focused. The rapid adoption of these technologies is reshaping how care is delivered, making healthcare more accessible, efficient, and effective. As this technological renaissance continues to unfold, both governments and investors are recognizing that the future of healthcare lies at the intersection of cutting-edge innovation and the urgent needs of a changing global population.

WHAT: Key Technologies Driving the Healthcare Revolution

The healthcare sector is being reshaped by a convergence of advanced technologies—AI, robotics, genomics, and telemedicine—just as the defense sector has been transformed by drones and quantum computing. These technologies are creating new possibilities for more precise diagnostics, personalized treatments, and more efficient healthcare delivery systems.

Quantum computing, in particular, is starting to play a crucial role by enabling complex molecular simulations for drug discovery and development, which traditional computers would take years to process. This capability is pivotal for modeling biochemical interactions at an unprecedented speed and scale, potentially reducing the time and cost associated with bringing new therapies to market.

- *AI in Healthcare:* AI's potential in healthcare goes far beyond data analysis. AI-powered systems are being deployed in hospitals and clinics to support diagnostics, predict patient outcomes, and improve surgical precision. From AI-driven imaging analysis that can detect cancers at earlier stages, through AI in drug development, to predictive algorithms that help manage hospital resources, AI is redefining care pathways and operational efficiency.

- *Quantum Computing in Healthcare:* Quantum computing is emerging as a transformative force in healthcare, particularly in the realms of drug discovery and personalized medicine. By leveraging its immense computational power, quantum computers can analyze vast datasets and perform complex molecular simulations in a fraction of the time it takes traditional supercomputers. This capability accelerates the development of new drugs and enables more precise genetic analysis, which could lead to highly personalized treatment plans and therapies.

- *Blockchain in Healthcare:* Blockchain technology is transforming how healthcare data is stored, shared, and secured. Blockchain's decentralized and tamper-proof ledger system ensures that patient records, medical histories, and genomic data remain secure and accessible only to authorized parties. This technology is also being applied in drug supply chains to ensure transparency and reduce the risk of counterfeiting.

- *Telemedicine and Remote Monitoring:* The pandemic
  made telemedicine mainstream, but its applications
  are expanding beyond remote doctor consultations.
  Telemedicine is now intertwined with wearable
  technologies that allow for continuous health
  monitoring, providing real-time data to healthcare
  providers. This convergence of telemedicine
  and wearable devices is enabling the long-term
  management of chronic conditions, empowering
  patients to take control of their health with minimal
  disruption to daily life.

- *Genomics and Personalized Medicine:* Genomics
  is revolutionizing healthcare by enabling the
  personalization of medical treatments based on
  an individual's genetic makeup. This shift toward
  personalized medicine allows for more targeted
  therapies, increasing efficacy and reducing side effects.
  Advances in genetic sequencing are also accelerating
  breakthroughs in oncology, rare disease treatments,
  and pharmacogenomics.

- *Robotics and Surgical Automation:* Robotics is playing
  an increasingly important role in precision surgeries.
  Robotic systems are being used to assist surgeons in
  performing delicate operations with greater accuracy,
  minimizing risks and recovery times for patients. These
  technologies, coupled with advancements in AI, are
  creating new frontiers in minimally invasive surgery.

- *Wearable Health Tech and Remote Monitoring:* The
  pandemic made telemedicine mainstream, but its
  applications are expanding beyond remote doctor
  consultations. Telemedicine is now intertwined

with wearable technologies like Apple Health and Fitbit, which allow for continuous health monitoring, providing real-time data to healthcare providers. This convergence enables the long-term management of chronic conditions, empowering patients to take control of their health with minimal disruption to daily life. AI-powered wearables can monitor vital signs such as heart rate and blood oxygen levels, offering insights that help prevent disease progression.

- *AI in Mental Health and Care Coordination:* AI's role in mental health is growing significantly, with companies like Woebot using AI-driven chatbots to provide therapy and support for mental health conditions. By leveraging large language models (LLMs), AI can assist in mental health diagnoses and improve access to care. Additionally, blockchain technology is enhancing mental health data privacy, ensuring that patients' sensitive mental health information is securely managed and shared only with authorized personnel.

- *AI in Drug Development and Biological Data Management:* AI is also revolutionizing drug discovery and development. Machine learning and deep learning techniques are being used by companies like Turbine and Certara to predict drug properties and optimize drug candidates, significantly reducing the time and cost of drug development. AI algorithms are also used to generate new molecules for potential drug candidates, speeding up the innovation pipeline.

WHO: The Private Sector's Role in Healthcare Innovation

Healthcare's Originators, Creative Destructors, Disruptive Innovators, and Beneficiaries are taking a leading role in the transformation of every corner of the vast healthcare vertical. While governments provide regulatory frameworks and funding, it is private companies that are driving innovation in critical areas such as AI, genomics, robotics, and quantum computing. Creative Destructors like Intuitive Surgical, which pioneered robotic surgery, and Illumina, a leader in genetic sequencing, are reshaping the healthcare landscape with groundbreaking products that enable more precise diagnostics and personalized treatments.

Startups are also playing a pivotal role in this transformation. Disruptive Innovators focused on AI-driven diagnostics, digital health platforms, and telemedicine solutions are seeing massive growth as the healthcare industry shifts toward more tech-driven, patient-centric models. The agility of the private sector allows these companies to rapidly innovate and anticipate healthcare needs before governments or large institutions can fully articulate them.

Qubit Pharmaceuticals, a European quantum computing startup, is utilizing quantum technology for drug discovery through its platform, Atlas. Designed to enhance the accuracy and precision of drug discovery and development, Atlas leverages quantum computing to enable developers to efficiently discover, optimize, and validate potential drug candidates by performing complex computational calculations in significantly reduced timeframes. In a bid to further accelerate drug discovery, Qubit Pharmaceuticals partnered with NVIDIA to create a hybrid computing platform.

Similarly, Polaris Quantum Biotech, a US-based company, is transforming the drug discovery process by combining quantum computing, artificial intelligence, and machine learning. Focused on

reducing the time needed to develop preclinical drug candidates, Polaris
Quantum Biotech offers Tachyon, a drug design platform capable
of optimizing multiple molecules at unprecedented speeds, making
significant strides in the efficiency of drug development.

Originators Leading the Public–Private Partnership to Leverage Transformative Technologies

A prime example of private sector innovation in healthcare is the
partnership between Originator IBM Quantum and Cleveland Clinic
launched in 2021. This groundbreaking collaboration aims to accelerate
biomedical discoveries through quantum computing, transforming drug
discovery, genomics, and personalized medicine. A key aspect of this
partnership is the installation of IBM's Quantum System One at Cleveland
Clinic, the first quantum computer to be housed at a healthcare institution,
enabling real-time medical research applications (Cleveland Clinic, 2021).

As Dr. Tom Mihaljevic, CEO and President of Cleveland Clinic,
highlighted: "Through this innovative collaboration, we have a unique
opportunity to explore quantum computing's potential to transform
healthcare, offering groundbreaking advancements in patient care
and research." He added that quantum computing has the potential to
revolutionize healthcare, making today's medical approaches seem as
outdated as bloodletting once did.

The partnership between Moderna and OpenAI marks a
groundbreaking advancement in drug discovery and mRNA vaccine
development. By combining Moderna's expertise in mRNA technology
with OpenAI's powerful artificial intelligence capabilities, the
collaboration aims to significantly accelerate the discovery and production
of new drugs. OpenAI's machine learning models will be used to analyze
vast amounts of biological data, identifying potential drug candidates
and optimizing the design of mRNA vaccines with unprecedented speed
and precision. This integration of AI into drug development promises to

enhance the efficacy of treatments, streamline the production process, and ultimately bring life-saving therapies and vaccines to market faster than ever before.

WHEN: Timing Considerations

Investing in healthcare technology requires careful consideration of timing due to the industry's conservative nature and extensive regulation. Barriers such as approvals from the FDA, compliance with HIPAA, GDPR standards, and stringent medical device regulations can significantly slow down the adoption of new technologies. These hurdles mean that even breakthrough innovations face long timelines before they can achieve widespread use.

For investors, it's important to be mindful of the Planning Fallacy, which highlights the tendency to underestimate the time needed to complete complex projects. The phenomenon, which was first proposed by psychologists Daniel Kahneman and Amos Tversky in 1979, highlights that despite the availability of historical data or personal experience suggesting otherwise, people consistently believe they can complete tasks faster and more efficiently than they realistically can.

Knowing about the Planning Fallacy and accompanying bias comes in handy when investors are looking to understand barriers to a particular technology's adoption. For example, the timing risk is lower for investing in technologies like AI for administrative tasks, diagnostic tools, or surgical robotics, as these are already being integrated into healthcare. However, investing in areas like genome sequencing or personalized medicine powered by quantum computing comes with a higher timing risk due to the early stages of development and the complexities involved.

While the timeline for mass adoption may be lengthy, that doesn't mean these technologies won't have a significant impact. Investors should focus on identifying signs that indicate the right time to invest, such as regulatory approvals, increasing adoption in healthcare institutions, or

strategic partnerships with established players. The timing risk varies
depending on the type of technology, so aligning your investment strategy
with where the industry stands on that adoption curve is essential.

HOW: Investment Strategies in Healthcare Technology

Investing in healthcare technology offers a variety of strategic approaches
that balance innovation with timing risks and industry challenges. Here
are just some of the many key strategies to consider:

- *Focus on Advanced Drug Development Technologies—
  more timing risk, but massive potential:* Invest in
  companies that are leveraging AI, quantum computing,
  blockchain, and genomics to accelerate drug discovery
  and development. These technologies are transforming
  how new drugs are identified, optimized, and brought
  to market, offering significant opportunities for long-
  term growth.

- *Prioritize Mature Technologies with Lower Timing
  Risks:* Technologies like AI for diagnostics, robotic
  surgery, and medical administration are already being
  integrated into healthcare, making them a lower-risk
  investment. These technologies are proving their value
  in clinical settings, offering near-term returns and a
  more stable entry point into healthcare innovation.

- *Invest in Data Integration and Interoperability-
  Ecosystem Infrastructure Play—lower risk:* As healthcare
  becomes more data-driven, investing in platforms that
  enable seamless integration of health data from various

sources is crucial. These systems will be essential for
advancing AI-driven diagnostics and personalized
medicine by ensuring that data can flow securely and
efficiently between healthcare providers.

- *Diversifying Across the HealthTech Ecosystem—lowest
  risk (timing and diversification, but returns will be
  averaged out):* For those seeking a broader, less hands-
  on approach, healthcare technology-focused ETFs
  or funds provide diversified exposure to multiple
  innovation sectors. This strategy helps spread risk while
  still capitalizing on advancements in AI, genomics, and
  digital health.

EXAMPLE 3: The Revolution in Manufacturing and Industry 5.0

WHY: Setting the Force Field Factor Stage

Manufacturing and supply chain management are undergoing a massive
transformation, driven by the convergence of revolutionary technologies.
These innovations are not just theoretical concepts—they are reshaping
factories, production lines, and global logistics in real time. This
technological revolution is now visibly unfolding in smart factories, where
AI-driven machines collaborate with human workers, making production
lines faster and more efficient than ever before.

A powerful example of this shift can be seen in Siemens' Amberg
plant, often referred to as one of the first fully operational "smart factories."
In this factory, nearly 75% of production processes are automated, with
AI and IoT technologies communicating across systems in real time to
optimize workflows. Helmut Schramm, head of the factory, has noted,

"The machines are talking to each other more than the humans are." This kind of real-time, AI-powered optimization is no longer a futuristic ideal but a present reality transforming how companies operate.

The COVID-19 pandemic and ongoing geopolitical tensions have exposed significant vulnerabilities in global supply chains. From sudden disruptions to challenges in maintaining transparency, these disruptions have prompted businesses to adopt advanced technologies at an accelerated pace. A 2021 McKinsey report found that nearly 85% of supply chain executives plan to implement digital technologies like AI and blockchain by 2025 to improve transparency and resilience. Blockchain, for instance, has revolutionized supply chain traceability, ensuring that every transaction—from raw materials to the final product—is secure and easily auditable. AI, on the other hand, helps predict potential bottlenecks, optimize routes, and streamline logistics to mitigate risk. As one supply chain executive from Unilever explained, "AI has transformed our ability to react to disruptions in real time, allowing us to keep our supply chain moving even during unprecedented challenges."

Robotics has brought an unparalleled level of precision to production lines, while IoT provides the crucial data streams necessary to connect every aspect of manufacturing. Much like in the defense and healthcare sectors, manufacturing is at a critical inflection point, where the race to digitize and automate has created a significant inflection point—driving a technological revolution that is reshaping the competitive landscape and creating immense investment opportunities.

Industry 5.0: Managing Workforce Shifts and Societal Impact

Industry 5.0 is redefining the intersection of technology and labor by focusing on human-centric approaches. Unlike Industry 4.0, which emphasized automation, Industry 5.0 fosters collaboration between humans and machines—merging human creativity with the precision of AI and collaborative robots (cobots). According to a report by PwC, automation could contribute up to $15 trillion to the global economy by 2030, but with this transformation comes challenges. While this shift promises increased efficiency and productivity, it also raises critical concerns about job displacement and income inequality, particularly in sectors like manufacturing and logistics, where machines could potentially replace entire roles. In fact, a 2020 report by McKinsey estimates that by 2030, as many as 375 million workers—or 14% of the global workforce—may need to switch occupational categories due to automation (McKinsey & Company, 2022).

In contrast, industries like healthcare and defense provide a different model. Here, technology enhances rather than replaces human roles. However, in manufacturing and logistics, the fear of obsolescence is far more acute, as automation poses a direct threat to many traditional jobs. A World Economic Forum report suggests that 85 million jobs could be displaced by automation by 2025, especially in these sectors (World Economic Forum, 2025).

This dynamic creates tension. Previous industrial revolutions displaced jobs with little regard for social consequences. This time, the impact could be more immediate, especially if workers feel excluded in a system that prioritizes technology over people. Surveys show that 25% of workers in the United States fear that their jobs will be automated within the next decade, according to a Pew Research Center study.

Industry 5.0 doesn't seek to eliminate jobs but to transform them. Machines will handle repetitive tasks, allowing humans to focus on more creative and strategic roles. However, this transformation demands substantial reskilling and upskilling efforts. The World Economic Forum estimates that 40% of workers will need reskilling by 2025 and 50% of all employees will need to upskill to stay competitive. Without adequate support, the risk of resistance is real, especially in economically vulnerable regions where workers fear being left behind. The challenge is not solely technological—it is also deeply social, requiring careful management to ensure that the benefits of this transformation are shared equitably.

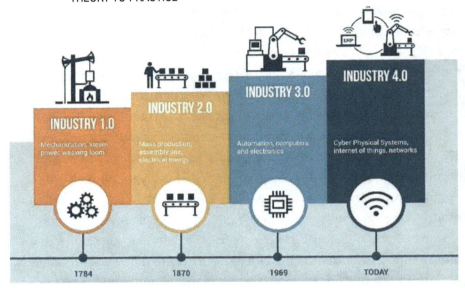

Figure 9-1. *The Evolution of Industrial Revolutions: This figure shows the progression from Industry 1.0 (mechanization and steam power, 1784) to Industry 4.0 (cyber-physical systems and IoT, today), highlighting key innovations like mass production (Industry 2.0) and automation (Industry 3.0) along a timeline*

WHAT: Key Technologies Driving Industry 5.0 and a Manufacturing Revolution

IoT and Blockchain: The Backbone of Smart Manufacturing

At the heart of Industry 4.0—the next generation of manufacturing—are IoT and blockchain technologies. IoT sensors are deployed across factory floors, embedded in machinery to gather real-time data on everything from machine health to production output. Imagine a network where every machine "talks" to its peers, adjusting its performance based on real-time data. These IoT-enabled devices can signal when a part needs

210

to be replaced before it fails, ensuring a smooth production process. This connectivity boosts productivity and enhances workplace safety by providing insights into machine conditions before any malfunctions occur.

Blockchain complements IoT by addressing critical concerns such as data security, integrity, and transparency. Every piece of data generated by IoT devices is stored securely on a blockchain ledger, making it tamper-proof. In this system, blockchain acts as the digital backbone that ensures transparency throughout the supply chain. For example, a car manufacturer can track the authenticity of each part in a vehicle, knowing exactly when and where it was produced. This decentralized system also allows manufacturers to implement smart contracts, which automatically enforce agreements between different parties. A supplier, for instance, can receive payment instantly when sensors confirm the delivery of goods.

These technologies work hand-in-hand to reduce inefficiencies, protect data from fraud, and allow manufacturers to respond to real-time changes. The benefits ripple across production lines and supply chains, creating systems that are more resilient, transparent, and secure.

AI and Robotics: Precision and Predictive Power

Artificial intelligence is transforming the decision-making processes within manufacturing, moving beyond human capabilities to predict issues before they occur. Take, for instance, AI-driven predictive maintenance systems that monitor machinery using IoT data. AI algorithms can detect subtle shifts in performance that human operators might miss, allowing for maintenance to be conducted before a costly breakdown. A smart factory could avoid weeks of downtime by preemptively replacing a single part based on AI forecasts. According to McKinsey, predictive maintenance powered by AI can reduce factory downtime by up to 50%, representing millions in potential savings.

Robotics further amplifies the power of AI by bringing unmatched precision and automation to manufacturing processes. Autonomous robots can be deployed to perform repetitive or dangerous tasks, such as assembling components in high-risk environments or moving heavy inventory across a warehouse. These robots, driven by AI, continually learn and adapt to the workflow, improving their efficiency with each task. For example, Amazon uses autonomous robots in its warehouses to transport products from storage to shipping, significantly reducing time and labor costs.

These AI and robotics technologies are optimizing everything from production schedules to logistics. AI-powered drones can be deployed to monitor inventory in real time, while robots handle the physical movement of goods, ensuring that production runs smoothly. The convergence of these systems allows for minimal human intervention, dramatically reducing the risk of error and increasing operational efficiency.

Supply Chain Management: Real-Time Decision-Making and Optimization

Supply chain management is undergoing a radical transformation, thanks to the integration of AI, blockchain, and IoT. The use of AI in supply chain management helps companies not only automate logistics but also make smarter, faster decisions. AI can analyze patterns in supply and demand, adjust inventory levels, and reroute goods when disruptions occur. By predicting market conditions and identifying inefficiencies in the supply chain, AI enhances agility and adaptability, ensuring that companies can keep up with ever-changing market dynamics.

Meanwhile, blockchain technology ensures that every step of the supply chain is transparent and traceable. Counterfeiting and fraud, which have long plagued the manufacturing industry, can be mitigated by blockchain's immutable ledger. Suppliers and manufacturers gain access to a shared, secure database, ensuring that materials are sourced responsibly and inventory is managed efficiently. With real-time visibility across the entire supply chain, companies can prevent disruptions and optimize operations to ensure smooth production flows.

IoT plays a critical role by providing the data necessary for AI to function effectively. Sensors on shipping containers, trucks, and factory floors collect real-time information about the location, temperature, and condition of goods. This data is fed into AI systems, enabling real-time decision-making and supply chain optimization. For example, if a shipment is delayed due to weather, the system can automatically reroute other shipments to prevent further disruption.

Together, AI, blockchain, and IoT form a powerful trio that is revolutionizing supply chain management. These technologies reduce costs, prevent fraud, and enhance visibility, giving companies the tools they need to navigate the complexities of global supply chains with confidence.

Integration with Emerging Technologies

The convergence of AI with other emerging technologies such as 5G, edge computing, and quantum computing is set to unlock new possibilities in manufacturing and supply chain management. These advancements will significantly enhance data processing capabilities and enable more complex, interconnected operations. For example, quantum computing's potential to solve highly complex optimization problems could revolutionize how manufacturers handle large-scale logistics and production planning. 5G will allow IoT devices to communicate faster and more reliably, further improving the efficiency of real-time data transfer in smart factories.

In addition, companies are already leveraging Web3 technologies like blockchain and smart contracts to enhance manufacturing logistics and supply chain processes. These technologies help track goods in real time, streamline customs clearance, reduce reliance on manual paperwork,

and minimize the risk of lost or stolen items. The intersection of AI
with these emerging technologies will give manufacturers new levels of
precision and agility, fundamentally changing how goods are produced,
tracked, and delivered.

Industry 5.0: A Human-Centric Shift

While the advancements of Industry 4.0 have revolutionized automation,
efficiency, and productivity in manufacturing, Industry 5.0 represents the
next evolutionary step. This new phase brings a human-centric approach
to manufacturing, focusing not just on workplace efficiency but also on
creating economic and social value. Industry 5.0 integrates advanced
technology with human creativity, placing greater emphasis on human
well-being and sustainability.

In Industry 5.0, humans and machines work alongside each other,
with robots and AI performing repetitive tasks while humans contribute
creativity, problem-solving, and emotional intelligence. This shift
aims to enhance workplace satisfaction and ensure that technological
advancements align with broader societal and environmental goals.
Companies are increasingly focusing on sustainability, ethical production,
and socially responsible business practices, all while incorporating
advanced technologies to support these goals.

Proactive Maintenance and Quality Control Management

IoT devices create a network that allows machines in a factory to
communicate continuously, sharing performance data that can be
analyzed by AI algorithms. This process creates a highly efficient system
of proactive maintenance, where potential equipment failures can
be predicted before they happen. Imagine a production line where
machines "self-diagnose" their issues—data is sent to AI systems, which

automatically schedule repairs or order replacement parts without human intervention. According to Deloitte, these predictive maintenance capabilities, enhanced by blockchain-secured data, can reduce downtime by up to 40%.

In a production environment where a single faulty component can halt operations, blockchain provides an immutable audit trail, tracking the quality and performance of each part. For instance, blockchain smart contracts can automate the verification of raw materials delivered by suppliers, triggering payments only when materials meet quality standards. If a batch of materials fails inspection, the blockchain system automatically initiates a process to return the goods, streamlining the quality control process and reducing costs.

In broader supply chain management, blockchain offers the transparency needed to combat counterfeiting and verify the origin of components. By 2025, Gartner predicts that blockchain could reduce supply chain costs by up to 30%, primarily by increasing transparency and reducing fraud, errors, and inefficiencies (Gartner Research, 2023).

WHO: The Companies Driving Industry 4.0 and 5.0

The coming Industry 5.0 era is being propelled by a mix of Originators, Disruptive Innovators, Creative Destructors, and Beneficiaries—each playing a pivotal role in integrating technologies like AI, blockchain, quantum computing, and IoT into the manufacturing ecosystem.

Originators Pioneering Technological Advancements:

- Companies like Arduino, MachineMetrics, Verusen, and Samsara are laying the foundation for Industry 5.0 by leveraging AI, IoT, and data analytics to optimize manufacturing and supply chains. These companies provide real-time monitoring, predictive analytics, and automation solutions that are critical to the future of smart factories.

215

- Established giants like Siemens AG, General Electric, Honeywell, and Bosch GmbH are integrating these advanced technologies into their wider business segments, positioning themselves as leaders in smart, automated manufacturing environments. While Industry 5.0 is just one piece of their operations, their success in this space could reshape their competitive edge in global markets.

Disruptive and Destructors:

- Universal Robots and ABB Robotics are leading the human-centric shift in manufacturing with cobots. These cobots work alongside humans, enhancing productivity while enabling safer and more efficient workplaces.

- Fathom is revolutionizing rapid prototyping and 3D printing, accelerating the shift toward on-demand manufacturing.

- VeChain is transforming supply chain transparency by integrating blockchain with IoT, ensuring secure, tamper-proof tracking of goods and materials.

- IBM and D-Wave are pushing the boundaries of quantum computing, enabling manufacturers to solve complex optimization problems and streamline operations on an unprecedented scale.

- Rockwell Automation and other integrators are essential to ensuring seamless implementation of Industry 5.0 technologies. Their role is crucial as manufacturers turn to experts to merge AI, IoT, blockchain, and robotics into existing operations, driving exponential growth in this space.

HOW: Investment Strategies for the Manufacturing Revolution

The convergence of IoT, AI, blockchain, robotics, 5G, and emerging technologies such as quantum computing presents investors with exciting opportunities. As in healthcare and defense, there are a number of smart strategies that one could employ. Here, we offer just a few to use as examples of how to participate in this vertical market:

- *Invest in Leading Integrators and Innovators:* As Industry 5.0 accelerates, it's crucial to focus on established firms and innovative startups that are integrating IoT, AI, blockchain, and robotics into manufacturing ecosystems. These players are driving the transformation of factories and supply chains into smart, interconnected systems. Investors should seek opportunities with organizations that are at the forefront of implementing cutting-edge technologies in manufacturing, offering potential for substantial long-term growth.

- *Focus on Human-Centric Enterprises:* With Industry 5.0 emphasizing a shift toward human-centric manufacturing, there is a growing demand for companies that integrate collaborative robotics and AI-driven human–machine collaboration. These companies focus on enhancing human roles rather than replacing them, creating workplaces where automation works alongside human creativity. Investors should look for businesses that prioritize not only technological innovation but also the well-being of workers and sustainable, ethical production practices.

- *Sustainability and ESG Investing:* Industry 5.0 is closely aligned with Environmental, Social, and Governance (ESG) goals, making sustainability-focused investing a key strategy. As manufacturers integrate advanced technologies, those that prioritize reducing waste, lowering carbon emissions, and embracing ethical sourcing practices are likely to gain prominence. Investing in companies that combine technological innovation with a focus on social and environmental responsibility will offer long-term value as sustainability becomes increasingly central to global business operations.

- *Leverage the Power of 5G and Edge Computing:* The rollout of 5G and edge computing is pivotal to the future of manufacturing. These technologies enable faster, more reliable real-time communication between IoT devices and AI systems, significantly improving the efficiency of smart factories and automated supply chains. Investors should consider opportunities with businesses that are leveraging 5G and edge computing to drive real-time data processing, predictive maintenance, and automation.

- *Diversification of Emerging Technologies:* The current strategies touch upon the most transformative technologies in Industry 5.0, but it might be beneficial to include other emerging trends like cybersecurity solutions. With IoT and AI adoption increasing, cybersecurity investments will become crucial in safeguarding interconnected manufacturing systems. A holistic strategy should account for protecting these innovations from potential cyber threats.

- *Risk Management and Resilience:* As global supply
  chains become more digital, investments in risk
  management technologies will grow. Companies
  that are resilient to disruptions, such as geopolitical
  instability or environmental disasters, will be more
  attractive. Investors should consider businesses that
  emphasize supply chain resilience through AI-driven
  forecasting and blockchain-enabled transparency.

WHEN: Timing Considerations and Corporate Roles

For investors, the question isn't just which technologies will transform the sector but when. Timing is crucial—some of these innovations are ripe for investment now, while others are still developing and require patience.

Among the most immediate opportunities is AI, which has matured into a practical, scalable tool for manufacturers. From predictive maintenance to supply chain optimization, AI is already delivering significant returns. Companies that integrate AI into their processes are seeing gains in efficiency, cost reduction, and real-time decision-making, making this a strong candidate for near-term investment. IoT, another key technology in Industry 5.0, has similarly reached a point where the investment case is compelling. The convergence of IoT with AI is creating more transparent and efficient supply chains, and as adoption of IoT solutions continues to expand, those investing in this space are likely to see solid returns.

Blockchain, while still emerging, is fast becoming an essential tool in supply chain management. Its ability to provide transparency and traceability is proving invaluable in industries where the provenance of materials is critical. While it may not yet be as mature as AI or IoT, blockchain's momentum is building, and it is increasingly being adopted to ensure supply chain integrity. This positions blockchain as a technology with strong medium-term growth potential.

However, not all Industry 5.0 technologies are ready for immediate investment. Quantum computing, though often touted as a game-changer, remains in the research and development phase. Its promise is immense, but quantum technology is still years away from practical application in manufacturing. Investors should approach quantum computing with caution, viewing it as a long-term play with high risk but potentially transformative rewards.

Similarly, while AI is already enhancing manufacturing processes, the vision of fully autonomous factories remains aspirational. Achieving true AI autonomy in industrial settings—where machines can operate with minimal human intervention—requires significant advances in robotics, machine learning, and real-time data processing. Though this is an exciting frontier, it will likely take several more years before such systems become viable at scale, making this a long-term investment area for those willing to wait.

Seizing the Moment: Investing at the Inflection Point of the Quantum Revolution

History has shown us that the biggest winners are those who recognize the larger landscape—those who see not just products but entire ecosystems and platforms being built. Just as industrialists harnessed the power of steam and electricity to build empires, today's visionary investors now have the rare chance to invest in the technology, infrastructure, and ecosystems that will fuel the future. The forces pushing us forward will only intensify, and the inflection points we are witnessing today—whether in AI-driven healthcare, quantum-powered drug discovery, or blockchain-secured supply chains—are just the beginning.

The Quantum Revolution represents more than technological progress; it's the next phase of human advancement. This is a once-in-a-generation opportunity, the moment where those who understand the seismic shift and invest strategically will help define the future. The window of opportunity is open now, but it won't last forever. The question is not if these technologies will reshape our world but who will be ready to leverage them at this critical inflection point.

APPENDIX A

Sources/Citations

Chapter 1

1. Calkin, J. and Karlsen, M (2014) Destination Imagination: Creativity in a World of Complacency, Journal of Applied Research on Children.

2. Rogers, E. M. (1962). Diffusion of Innovations. Free Press of Glencoe.

3. Moore, G. A. (1991). Crossing the Chasm: Marketing and Selling High-Tech Products to Mainstream Customers. Harper Business.

4. Gartner Research. (2023). Understanding Gartner's Hype Cycles. Gartner, Inc.

5. U.S. Census Bureau. (1975). Historical Statistics of the United States: Colonial Times to 1970.

6. International Telecommunications Union. (2023). Global ICT Statistics.

7. GSMA Intelligence. (2023). The Mobile Economy Report.

8. Boston Consulting Group. (2023). The Race for Quantum Computing Advantage.

9. World Economic Forum. (2023). Technology Adoption Trends Report.

10. O'Reilly. (2023). Cloud Adoption in 2023.

11. Fortinet. (2021). Cloud Security Report.

12. DataReportal. (2024). Digital Global Overview Report.

13. Statista Digital Market Outlook. (2024). Worldwide Internet User Forecast.

14. U.S. Department of Energy. (2022). Historical Electricity Usage Patterns.

15. Mecke, J. (2021) How Has Technology Adoption Life Cycle Been Shortened in 2021.

16. Bussgang, J. (2021) After 30 years, "Crossing the Chasm" is due for a refresh.

17. Hughes, T. P. (1983). Networks of Power: Electrification in Western Society, 1880–1930. Johns Hopkins University Press.

18. Israel, P. (1998). Edison: A Life of Invention. John Wiley & Sons.

19. Carlson, W. B. (2013). Tesla: Inventor of the Electrical Age. Princeton University Press.

20. Lague, D. (2023). U.S. and China race to shield secrets from quantum computers. Reuters.

21. Turing, A., 1950, "Computing Machinery and Intelligence," Mind.

Chapter 2

1. Gordon, J. S. (1989). Edison and the Electric Light: A Study in Discovery and Innovation. American Heritage.

Chapter 3

1. Amara, R. (1978). Brief history of forecasting and futures studies. Institute for the Future.

2. Bloomberg New Energy Finance & National Human Genome Research Institute. (2023). Technology Cost Curves: Comparative Analysis of Emerging Technologies. BNEF & NHGRI Joint Report.

3. Intel Corporation. (2022). 50 Years of Moore's Law: Transistor Density and Computing Performance. Intel Technology Journal.

4. Kurzweil, R. (2005). The Singularity Is Near: When Humans Transcend Biology. Viking Press.

5. Metcalfe, R. (1995). Metcalfe's Law: A network becomes more valuable as it reaches more users. Infoworld, 17(40), 53–54.

6. Metcalfe, R., & Gilder, G. (2013). Metcalfe's Law and Network Effects: A Critical Evaluation and Application. Journal of Telecommunications Policy, 37(10), 751-761.

7. Moore, G. E. (1965). Cramming more components onto integrated circuits. Electronics Magazine, 38(8), 114–117.

8. NASA Historical Archives & Apple Inc. (2023). Comparative Computing Capabilities: From Space Exploration to Modern Smartphones. Technology Evolution Report.

9. Morgan Stanley Research. (2023). Technology Adoption Acceleration: Historical Trends and Modern Patterns. Morgan Stanley Global Investment Research.

10. Rose, G. (2014). Quantum Computing and Moore's Law. D-Wave Systems Technical Publications.

Chapter 4

1. BlackRock Investment Report. (2023). "The Future of Digital Assets and Blockchain Technology".

2. Preskill, J. (2012): Quantum Computing and the Entanglement Frontier.

3. Capital One Annual Reports (1995–2000).

4. McKinsey & Company. (2020). "How COVID-19 has pushed companies over the technology tipping point—and transformed business forever".

5. "The Impact of Mobile Technology" by Morgan Stanley Research (2023).

6. Georgieva, K., et al. (2024). "Gen-AI: Artificial Intelligence and the Future of Work." IMF Staff Report.

7. Arute, F., et al. (2019). Quantum supremacy using a programmable superconducting processor. Nature, 574(7779), 505-510..

Chapter 5

1. ARK Invest. (2024). Big Ideas 2024 Report: Technological Convergence and Market Projections.

2. PwC. (2024). Essential Eight Technologies Report Update.

3. IBM. (2023). Global AI Adoption Index.

4. Harvard Business Review. (2023). Digital Transformation and Technology Convergence.

6. Microsoft Research. (2023). The Future of Mixed Reality and Virtual Collaboration.

Chapter 6

1. Rogers, E. M. (2003). Diffusion of Innovations (5th ed.). Free Press.

2. Christensen, C. M. (2015). The Innovator's Dilemma. Harvard Business Review Press.

3. Schumpeter, J. A. (1942). Capitalism, Socialism and Democracy. Harper & Brothers.

4.   ARK Invest. (2024). "Big Ideas 2024 Report: Technology Convergence Analysis."

5.   PwC. (2024). "Essential Eight Technologies: 2024 Update."

6.   Gartner Research. (2023). "Technology Lifecycle Management Framework."

7.   McKinsey Global Institute. (2024). "Creative Destruction in the Digital Era."

8.   Bernstein Research. (2024). "AirPods Market Analysis and Valuation."

9.   IDC. (2024). "Global Device Tracker: PC Market Evolution."

10. Bloomberg Financial Markets. (2024). "NVIDIA Market Performance Analysis 2016-2024."

11. Morgan Stanley. (2024). "Apple Product Line Valuation Report."

12. RIAA. (2024). "Annual Music Industry Revenue Report."

13. Digital Entertainment Group. (2024). "Streaming Market Share Analysis."

14. Apple Inc. (2024). Annual Report FY2023.

15. NVIDIA Corporation. (2024). Annual Report FY2023.

16. Netflix Inc. (2000–2024). Shareholder Letters.

17. Spotify Technology S.A. (2023). Annual Report.

18. Harvard Business Review. (2023). "Apple's Technology Maturation Strategy."

19. MIT Technology Review. (2024). "Technology Lifecycle Patterns."

20. World Economic Forum. (2024). "The Future of Technology Report."

21. Galloway, S. (2024). "Second Mouse.AI Newsletter: Disruptive Innovation Analysis."

22. Kennedy, J. F. (1963). Address at Assembly Hall, Frankfurt, Germany. June 25, 1963.

Media Industry Data

23. Journal of Innovation Management. (2024). "Patterns of Creative Destruction in Digital Markets." Vol. 12(1), pp. 45–67.

24. Morgan Stanley Research (2024). Technology Maturation in Consumer Electronics.

Chapter 7

1. IBM Quantum Experience statistics (IBM Annual Report, 2024).

2. Airbnb market impact data (Hospitality Industry Report, 2024).

3. NVIDIA AI market growth (Bloomberg Financial Markets, 2024).

4. Vision Pro and Metaverse market statistics (Morgan Stanley Research, 2024).

5. Nadella, S. (2015). Microsoft Build Developer Conference Keynote.

6. Ford, H. (1922). Ford Motors Company Archives.

7. Zuckerberg, M. (2009). Facebook F8 Developer Conference.

8. Bezos, J. (2015). Amazon Annual Shareholder Letter.

9. Jobs, S. (1997). Apple Worldwide Developers Conference.

10. Christensen, C. M. (1997). The Innovator's Dilemma.

11. Drucker, P. (1985). Innovation and Entrepreneurship.

12. Schumpeter, J. A. (1942). Capitalism, Socialism and Democracy.

13. Morgan Stanley. (2024). "Technology Sector Analysis: AR/VR Market."

Chapter 8

1. McKinsey & Company. "The Economic Potential of Generative AI: The Next Frontier." McKinsey Global Institute, 2023.

Chapter 9

1. Stockholm International Peace Research Institute (SIPRI). "Trends in World Military Expenditure." SIPRI Report, 2023.

2. World Economic Forum. "The Future of Jobs Report." WEF, 2025.

3. McKinsey & Company. "Global Supply Chains: The Road to Resilience." McKinsey Global Institute, 2022.

4. Gartner. "AI in Supply Chain: Emerging Practices." Gartner Research, 2023.

5. Cleveland Clinic. "Quantum Computing in Healthcare Research." Press Release, 2021.

6. Lighthouse. (2023). Industry 4.0 to Pharma 4.0: Evolution of the Industrial Revolutions.

Embracing the Quantum Revolution—A Historic Opportunity

"Somewhere, something incredible is waiting to be known. It is the tension between the certainty and the mystery that makes the future so fascinating and so perilous." Carl Sagan's emphasis on the beauty of the unknown, juxtaposed against the reality of the dangers and challenges humanity faces in pursuing progress, is a microcosm of what *Investing in Revolutions: Creating Wealth from Transformational Technology Waves* attempts to accomplish for its readers.

The chapters have traversed the complex journeys of our most epic technological revolutions, from their nascent stages, the explosive heights of mainstream adoption, and their extinctions as they make way for another life-changing wave. But what lies ahead is not merely a continuation of past trends; it is an unprecedented opportunity to participate in shaping the future.

© Tal Elyashiv 2025
T. Elyashiv, *Investing in Revolutions*, https://doi.org/10.1007/979-8-8688-1177-7

The Quantum Revolution is not just another phase in technological advancement; it is a paradigm shift that promises to redefine the very fabric of our industries, impacting everything from the pills we swallow to the policies we enact. From healthcare to finance, from education to manufacturing, the ripple effects of this revolution will be profound and all-encompassing.

We live in an era where the most valuable investment may not lie in the technologies themselves but in understanding the human behaviors that shape their use. The real winners are those who grasp not only the patterns of technological adoption but also the underlying social and economic shifts. It's as much about anticipating human nature as it is about betting on hardware and software. At the same time, we face a period of profound societal, economic, and political transformation, marked by uncertainty and upheaval. In these turbulent times, the insights in this book are more crucial than ever. Mastering the cycle of technological evolution, identifying the signs of emerging trends, and distinguishing real opportunities from hype are the skills that will empower both investors and innovators.

This book is not merely an investment guide; it is a compass that offers the right mix of vision and insight needed to anticipate what's ahead and then make decisions to stay ahead. It's a vista not just of graphs and numbers but of people, patterns, and passions. It leverages historical context to illuminate the paths forward, ensuring that we are not just passive observers but active participants in the unfolding technological narrative. The convergence of technologies like AI, blockchain, and quantum computing is not just enabling opportunities for wealth creation; it is inviting us to be part of a transformation that will redefine how we live, work, and interact.

As we look ahead, the principles outlined in this book will serve as enduring guides. The ability to adapt, the foresight to see beyond the horizon, and the wisdom to make informed decisions will be more critical than ever. Personally, I've spent the last eight years predicting, pioneering, participating, and as a result benefiting handsomely from one of the pillars of the quantum revolution—blockchain technology. Envisioning the maturation and convergence of AI, blockchain, and quantum computing and their transformative power for humanity, I urge you to join me and others in this exciting journey over the next couple of decades riding the quantum revolution.

For those prepared to embrace the challenges and opportunities of this new era, the rewards will be substantial. In this revolution, as in all others, knowledge remains the most potent currency. Equip yourself with it, and let's create, invest, and inspire the future we imagine.

Index

© Tal Elyashiv 2025
T. Elyashiv, *Investing in Revolutions*, https://doi.org/10.1007/979-8-8688-1177-7

C

D

E

V

W, X, Y, Z

www.ingramcontent.com/pod-product-compliance
Lightning Source LLC
LaVergne TN
LVHW051638050326
832903LV00022B/800